MELANIN
BASE CAMP

MELANIN
BASE CAMP

REAL-LIFE ADVENTURERS BUILDING A
MORE INCLUSIVE OUTDOORS

Danielle Williams

BLACK DOG
& LEVENTHAL
PUBLISHERS
NEW YORK

Cover design by Katie Benezra
Cover photographs by Irene Yoo
Cover copyright © 2023 by Hachette Book Group, Inc.

Black Dog & Leventhal Publishers
Hachette Book Group
1290 Avenue of the Americas
New York, NY 10104
www.hachettebookgroup.com
www.blackdogandleventhal.com

First edition: March 2023

Melanin Base Camp® is a registered trademark.

Black Dog & Leventhal Publishers is an imprint of Perseus Books, LLC, a subsidiary of Hachette Book Group, Inc. The Black Dog & Leventhal Publishers name and logo are trademarks of Hachette Book Group, Inc.

The publisher is not responsible for websites (or their content) that are not owned by the publisher.

The Hachette Speakers Bureau provides a wide range of authors for speaking events. To find out more, go to www.HachetteSpeakersBureau.com or call (866) 376-6591.

Photo credits are on page 240.

Print book interior design by Katie Benezra

Library of Congress Cataloging-in-Publication Data
Names: Williams, Danielle, author.
Title: Melanin Base Camp : real-life adventurers pushing the boundaries of inclusion and equity in the great outdoors / Danielle Williams.
Description: First edition. | New York : Black Dog & Leventhal, 2022. | Includes bibliographical references.
Summary: "Part SHE EXPLORES and part BLACK FUTURES, MELANIN BASE CAMP explores the many different ways people of color experience the outdoors through inspiring photographs, in-depth interviews, and essays, all that challenge readers to rethink their perceptions of what an outdoorsy individual looks like" —Provided by publisher.
Identifiers: LCCN 2021053572 (print) | LCCN 2021053573 (ebook) | ISBN 9780762479320 (hardcover) | ISBN 9780762479337 (ebook)
Subjects: LCSH: Outdoor recreation—Social aspects—United States. | Outdoor life—Social aspects—United States. | African Americans—Recreation. | Minorities—United States—Recreation. | Melanin Base Camp (Organization)
Classification: LCC GV191.4 .W545 2022 (print) | LCC GV191.4 (ebook) | DDC 796.50973--dc23/eng/20211207
LC record available at https://lccn.loc.gov/2021053572
LC ebook record available at https://lccn.loc.gov/2021053573

ISBNs: 978-0-7624-7932-0 (hardcover); 978-0-7624-7933-7 (ebook)

Printed in Singapore

COS

10 9 8 7 6 5 4 3 2 1

Contents

Introduction

HELLO, MY NAME IS DANIELLE WILLIAMS. I'M AN AFRICAN AMERICAN skydiver, blogger, and the founder of Melanin Base Camp. While I grew up trail running, my love for adventure sports began in 2006 when the United States Army threw me out of my first airplane. Five years later, I became a licensed skydiver, and since then, I've spent the past decade hiking, camping, and hucking gainers out of tailgate aircraft on warm summer afternoons.

Community is such an important part of outdoor spaces. While it's true that many people "escape" to the outdoors to get away from the hustle and bustle of everyday life, it's equally true that entire communities—both in-person and online—have sprung up around our shared love of outdoor activities, ranging from gardening to thru-hiking to BASE jumping. Let's face it; we like being outside . . . together! Unfortunately, truly inclusive communities are sometimes hard to find and being "the only one" can be exhausting. Yet, if you are a Person of Color trying to get outside and stay active, that is often your starting point.

In 2014, I co-founded Team Blackstar Skydivers, an online affinity space, to provide community for other skydivers of Color; that was followed by outdoor diversity blog Melanin Base Camp in 2016 and, shortly thereafter, Diversify Outdoors, a coalition of digital influencers, activists, nonprofits, and allies committed to building a more equitable outdoors.

When I first began thinking critically about the lack of diversity in the outdoors, my goal was to increase the participation of other racial minorities. There was only one problem with that. The more research I did, the more I realized that we already surf, hike, bike, climb, and paddle—all things I assumed People of Color didn't do. That was a good lesson to learn. I didn't know because I had never seen any images of Senegalese surfers, queer Latinx climbers, or Asian thru-hikers. At the time, I couldn't recall a single U.S. outdoor retailer featuring an adventure athlete of Color in a nationally televised ad. So, I assumed we didn't exist. But I was wrong!

These days, social media tells a different story. Photo-sharing apps like Instagram, where #MelaninBaseCamp and #DiversifyOutdoors have been used over 50K and 100K times respectively, allow us to connect, ask questions, share knowledge, and create our own narratives, one video at a time. Anyone who has ever watched Chloe Kim nail back-to-back 1080s in the half-pipe or watched Dominique Miller *noseriding*

her longboard off Queen's Break knows that images are powerful. They influence the stories we tell about ourselves and the people we aspire to become. Melanin Base Camp is our story. We are strong, empowered, and resilient. We care about our communities, and we care about conserving public lands. We're passing on our love of the outdoors to the next generation, and we realize that representation matters.

So, here's our new goal—to increase the visibility of adventurous People of Color and to increase our representation in the media, in advertising, and, most importantly, in the stories we tell ourselves about the outdoors.

Whether you hike, climb, bike, or paddle, Melanin Base Camp is your home too. Join the movement and help us #DiversifyOutdoors!

Land Acknowledgment

I'M EXCITED TO SHARE THE STORIES OF TWENTY-FOUR REAL-LIFE adventurers of Color who are pursuing their passion in the outdoors and giving back to their communities. The people whose stories line these pages are diverse in many ways, but we have this in common—we are all survivors. Collectively, our ancestors survived the trauma of immigration, the trauma of the trans-Atlantic slave trade, and the trauma of residential schools and stolen land. By hiking, trail running, foraging, and more, we are forging new relationships with the outdoors while reconnecting with old traditions. Our cultures have always been tied to the land.

Before I go further, it's important that we take a moment to acknowledge whose land we're recreating on. Many of these stories take place in national and state parks across the United States. Public land is Native land. The United States is Native land. That goes beyond the 574 federally recognized tribes to encompass tribes that are fighting for recognition. It also includes Alaska Natives, Native Hawaiians, First Nations, and other Indigenous people whose ancestral land is split by U.S. borders.

Land acknowledgments are not enough; however, they're a good place to start. Learn the history of the land you're recreating on. Learn about the culture and the people whose land you're recreating on. Support Native-led activism and remember: The outdoors is not a playground; neither is it a pristine wilderness. It is a home—and has been a home to Indigenous people for millennia. They are still here.

I hope that this inspires you to think about your own ancestors and where they came from, whether they are indigenous to the United States or not. My own ancestors were stolen from West Africa and brought to Turtle Island centuries ago, where they were enslaved for generations on Santee land in South Carolina. My own history is a personal reminder that Black and Indigenous liberation is not separate. It has always been bound together.

Regardless of how you identify, we encourage you to use the Native Land app to learn more about whose land you're recreating on.

Guide to Outdoor Allyship: Part 1

PRIVILEGE

WHAT DOES PRIVILEGE HAVE TO DO WITH THE OUTDOORS? A LOT, actually. Nature is inhabited by people who reflect the same biases you see everywhere in society. While it's tempting to view the outdoors as a transcendent experience that will smooth over unpleasant topics like police brutality and racism, that's more wishful thinking than reality. Forest bathing doesn't wash away bigotry. John Muir quotes do nothing to resolve racial inequality.

Privilege is hard to see. In fact, the more you have it, the less likely you are to be aware that it exists. For example, if you are an able-bodied, gender-conforming white person, you benefit from multiple forms of discrimination—even if you don't want to; even if your intentions are good; even if you try your best to treat others how you would like to be treated.

Privilege sounds like the insistence that you don't see race or the belief that you can be queer without "getting all political." It looks like the ability to compartmentalize or "shut up and climb" because certain forms of discrimination don't affect you.

Is it possible to use your privilege for good? The short answer is yes. If you are white and queer, you can use your privilege to speak up without fear of harassment in spaces where queer People of Color are attacked or ignored for expressing the same opinion. If you are a cisgender man of Color, you absolutely have a role to play in dismantling systems that deliberately silence and disenfranchise women and femmes of Color. If you are non-disabled, you can support the leadership and activism of disabled people. If you are white and transgender, you can use your privilege to the amplify the voices of trans People of Color.

Acknowledging privilege requires us to first turn inward and recognize that even though we may face discrimination in certain areas of our life, there may be other areas where we benefit from the oppression of others—and being nice won't fix it.

A Chosen Family of Complete Strangers

featuring Danielle Williams

TURTLE ISLAND

SANTEE

I KNEW THREE THINGS GROWING UP: THAT I'D ATTEND A MILITARY academy like my father, that I'd be a lifelong runner like my mother, and that I'd accomplish whatever I set out to do in life—just like the big-haired, spandex-clad heroines leaping off the pages of the science-fiction novels that I read as a kid. They were fearless. I aspired to be also.

Life didn't exactly work out as planned. It's true, I watched from the bleachers as my uniform-clad siblings tossed their hats in the air on graduation day at West Point, and it's also true that I stopped running after a long-term illness, but I haven't stopped pursuing my dreams even as they've gradually changed over time.

I no longer want to conquer the world. I want to make smaller changes instead. One of those small changes has been to encourage People of Color to take up more space in the outdoors.

In 2011, I learned how to skydive. I was chasing an "alive" feeling and I found it in the exhilaration that comes from free-falling 13,000 feet and taking

your life into your own hands! I took my parachute rig with me and jumped all over the United States, as well as in Thailand and the Philippines. I camped out at drop zones and slept in strangers' cabins and pitched my tent in the woods. At age twenty-five, I did a trust fall into the skydiving community and had no regrets.

In California, I slept in a stranger's camper along with several other skydivers. Each morning, we stumbled out into the chilly air, lured by the aroma of fried eggs, toast, and coffee percolating on the Jetboil. Jumping was secondary to sharing our life stories, which spanned several continents and languages.

In the Northeast, I rose before sunrise to plunge 10,000 ft from a hot air balloon—a tradition I would repeat several times over the same sleepy Pennsylvania countryside. I loved bracing against the cold, marveling at how quietly and quickly the balloon carried us aloft, and steeling myself for the way my heart leapt into my throat with each "dead air" drop.

In the Pacific Northwest, I did my first night jump—on accident. After a slow climb to altitude in a small aircraft while circling a brand new-to-me drop zone, I was surprised to see the beautiful sunset eclipsed by fog and darkness. "Don't worry, there's a blinking light on the airfield," the instructor said right before the blinking light on the airfield blinked out. Thankfully, the other jumpers on the ground improvised, using their vehicles and headlights to guide us safely back to earth—safely but not elegantly. I ran out my landing and slid feet-first underneath the bumper of a parked Jeep, its KC lights fully ablaze, to the horror of onlookers.

In the Southeast, long, hot summer days of skydiving were followed by Low Country boils spread out on picnic tables lined with newspaper and skinny-dipping in nearby lakes. Beer bottles clinking as soon as the happy hour light came on, signaling the end of jump operations for the day.

Skydiving means a chosen family of complete strangers. It means the same language no matter where I travel in the globe and no matter what language is spoken. Our gear is the same, our preparations for each dive are the same, and we flash the same shaka signs before climbing out onto the strut and dropping into blue sky.

It's not that bad things don't happen; they do. There have been times when I felt unsafe as a Black woman traveling alone to drop zones in rural areas. I also found that people are quick to make assumptions about my ability, experience level, and technical knowledge, based solely on the color of my skin. When I visit new drop zones, I am routinely mistaken for a tandem customer despite the obvious signs: a gear bag and parachute on my back and my helmet in hand. It reinforces the fact that many people will never see me as a "real skydiver" because, in their minds, "Black people don't skydive!" That's a hard truth that bothered me less when I was a newcomer but can really get under my skin as an experienced jumper with hundreds of skydives and over a decade in the sport.

Drop zones are also places where sexist, homophobic, and racist language is often met with laughter, or averted glances from allies who are too afraid to speak up. The truth is our community shares the same "bro" culture as

many other adventure sports. Despite this, I believe we have a lot of potential to be a diverse, accepting, and inclusive community.

I've been skydiving for over a decade, and I don't regret the decision. I love taking the camera step on a jump so I can capture video for a newly licensed skydiver who is eager to share their world with their family and friends. It's a way of paying it forward, because there were people who did the same for me when I was brand new. I love skydiving traditions, like beer for first-time offenses and pieing skydivers on their hundredth and thousandth jumps. I love the rush that comes from successfully completing a dive plan and the preternaturally calm organizers who help us achieve the impossible in the sky.

I also no longer get super stressed when things don't work out as planned.

Skydiving taught me that. I've landed at Walmart and in cow pastures, cornfields, alfalfa fields, soccer fields—you name it—if it's a type of field, I've probably landed in it. Life has a way of unraveling the best-laid plans.

Since I began skydiving, I've started things and not finished them, like my pilot's license after I got sick. I've slowed down—a lot—since becoming disabled, and that no longer makes me feel as anxious or upset. Sometimes it feels really unfair that I no longer have access to the things that gave me a sense of peace—like distance running or putting in long hours at the drop zone every weekend, but I still jump and have started hiking a lot more with my elbow crutches, when my body feels up to it. When I can't do that, I plant my feet in the grass and slip a little Maker's Mark into my hot tea, and that counts too.

The purpose of this book is not to convince you to hike, climb, paddle, or skydive but to show you that good things await on the other side of uncertainty and self-doubt—if this is something you're interested in. It's scary to try new experiences—especially when you don't have all the details and especially if you're the only person who looks like you. The outdoors is truly for everyone. Just remember to go at your own pace and as far as you feel comfortable going. Don't mistake anyone else's journey for your own.

Learning
How to Fall

featuring Dr. Favia Dubyk

ALBUQUERQUE, NEW MEXICO
TIGUA (TIWA), PIRO, PUEBLOS

DR. FAVIA DUBYK IS A THIRTY-FIVE-YEAR-OLD PHYSICIAN, CANCER survivor, and professional rock climber. The former collegiate sprinter studied environmental science and public policy at Harvard, where she also set a school record in the women's 100-meter race, before she learned to climb. A few years later, Favia was attending medical school in Cleveland and dating "a cute guy" when she suddenly began experiencing fatigue and difficulty breathing. After a battery of tests and the discovery of a 13-cm mass in her chest, she was diagnosed with non-Hodgkin's lymphoma.

The diagnosis upended her life. She suffered through a major surgery and several life-threatening medical complications, including collapsed lungs and fluid around her heart before she was able to start chemotherapy. Eventually, Favia recovered, married that cute guy, and completed medical school. She also began climbing again.

Regaining her strength took time, but climbing soon became a central part of her life. "My favorite part of climbing is the sensation of having my life hanging from my fingertips," Favia described thoughtfully. She climbs V12 boulders, mostly lowball roofs where she can fall a short distance onto her back and the crash pad below, without fear of injury.

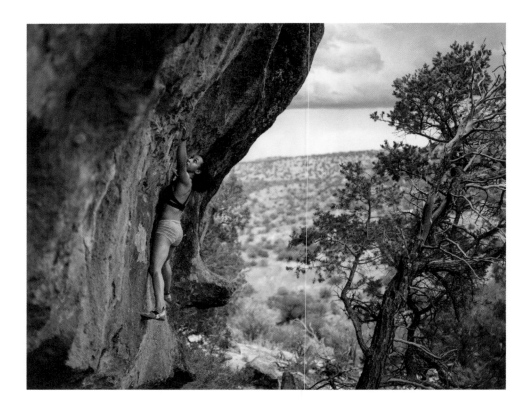

She has Ehlers-Danlos syndrome and is prone to painful partial dislocations called *joint subluxations*.

Bouldering is a type of rock climbing that doesn't require a harness or ropes. "With bouldering, all I need is my dog, shoes, and a crash pad," she explained. The minimal requirements have allowed her to climb around her busy schedule as a physician. The sport requires incredible core and finger strength, and its trial-and-error process appeals to the former Division I athlete. On social media, she posts photos of her lean, muscular 5'2" frame suspended from "barely there" granite holds or hanging upside down from toe hooks.

She also loves the short bursts of movement that differentiate bouldering from other types of climbing. "I know a lot of people like to climb to gain vertical height, or to get views," said Favia. "I climb because I like the movement."

Year-round, she mostly climbs at night to escape the desert heat in New Mexico, where she lives with her husband, crag dog Hans, and five cats. That has become more and more important as her skill level has progressed. "At harder grades, the holds get so small that you need every advantage possible," Favia explained. "You don't want sweaty hands or wet rock. Even the rubber on your climbing shoes has an ideal temperature for generating the most friction." While she prefers 30°F to 40°F, she's been known to climb in 15°F weather with earmuffs and booties.

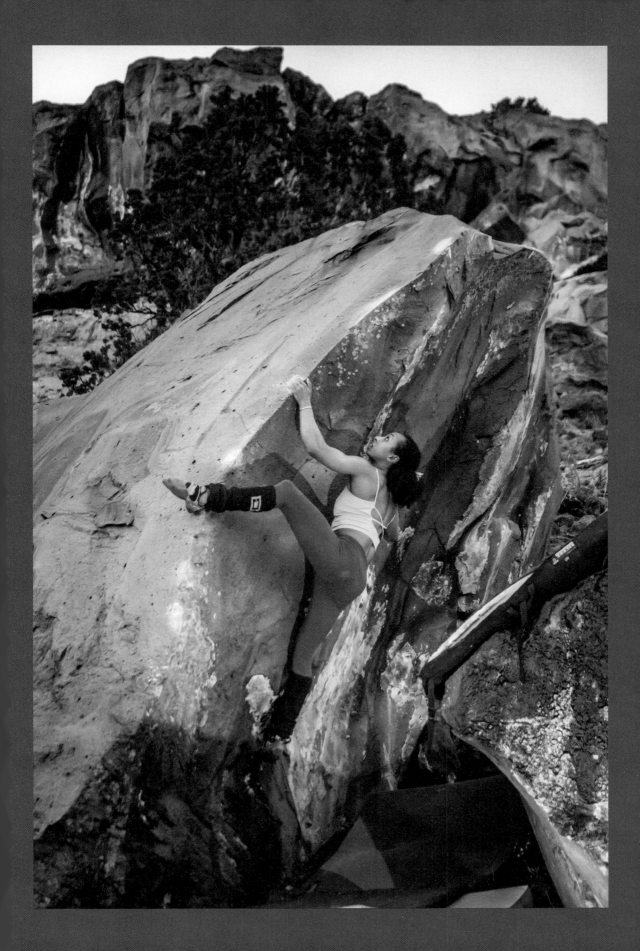

Her nighttime sessions boosted her mental health during her residency and fellowship as she dealt with racism, misogyny, and a toxic work environment. "During that time, I needed climbing to get through the next day," Favia recalled. These days, she actually finds herself climbing less and incorporating more rest days.

Bouldering has also challenged her to face her fears on and off the rock. In the past few years, Favia has worked with a sports counselor to help her overcome her fear of dislocating joints and to get comfortable with riskier, more dynamic movement. Her efforts have paid off: "I never thought I'd be climbing double digits with hard moves twenty feet off the ground!" she said enthusiastically. "It's been a long road."

She also competed in seasons 10 and 11 of *American Ninja Warrior*. "I'm currently training for my first professional competition, called Tuck Fest," said Favia. "You climb forty-five feet without a rope and then fall into the water." She's tackling her fear by doing as much preparation as possible, including jumping off cliffs and taking swimming lessons to increase her comfort level in the water. "I know in the moment on the wall, I'll still be afraid," she added. "The goal is to be confident in your skills so that when fear creeps in, it doesn't matter."

Running for Healing and Social Change

featuring Verna Volker

MINNEAPOLIS, MINNESOTA

WAHPEKUTE, OČHÉTHI ŠAKÓWIŊ

WHEN VERNA VOLKER FIRST BEGAN RUNNING, SHE WAS A MOTHER OF three living in Minneapolis, Minnesota, far from the Navajo (Diné) reservation where she grew up. She and her husband were brand-new to the community, and Verna couldn't help but notice the nearby lake and miles of trails. "I also remember thinking that I was taking care of everybody except for myself," Verna recalled. So she decided to go for a run. That decision was life-changing. Verna ran for a few miles and thought, "I really like this." Not long after, she signed up for her first half marathon. By the end of the race, she was hooked on running. That was thirteen years ago, and the forty-eight-year-old ultrarunner shows no signs of stopping. She's currently training for her first 100K (62-mile) race.

Running boosted her confidence and helped her tackle new goals and distances, but the change didn't happen overnight. "I like to remind people that it was a slow progression," said Verna. After having a daughter in 2016, she ran several 50K (31-mile) races, followed by her first 50 miler.

Finding time to train for long-distance runs between taking care of four kids isn't easy. She sticks to early morning workouts in order to minimize the disruption to her kids' schedules. On the weekend, that means waking up at 2:45 a.m. in order to hit the trail by 4:00 a.m. with a headlamp. For the most part, she runs alone. "Oftentimes people will ask, how can you be out there for eight hours by yourself?" Verna laughed. "I always have people around me, including my kids, so I guess I just enjoy the alone time."

It's not uncommon for Verna to run an entire marathon during a weekend training run. The long solo runs are about so much more than building mileage or working toward a new personal best. Running has become a way for her to process loss. "I've dealt with a lot of grief and trauma in my life, including the loss of three siblings and my father at a young age," Verna explained. "I always dedicate miles to someone by writing their name on my shoe. When it gets difficult at the 25-mile point, that keeps me going." Ultrarunning has evolved from a way to prioritize her health to a means of promoting healing and resilience.

Running also keeps Verna connected to her heritage. As a child growing up in rural New Mexico, she spent a lot of time outdoors. "My playground was the cañónes, the mesas," Verna recalled. "My favorite part was the smell of sagebrush after it rained." Even though moving to Minneapolis meant leaving that behind, trail running is a reminder that she belongs outside.

In 2016, Verna joined Instagram and began looking for a community of Native runners. In a sport that has long been defined by the promotion of thin, white runners in popular media, it was difficult to find other people who looked like her. "I remember thinking, 'that's not me' and 'there has to be other people who feel the way I do,'" Verna recalled. "I started to wonder, 'where's my place in running—where do I fit in?'"

In the absence of an online community, Verna created one. In January 2018, she founded Native Women Running on Instagram. On her popular account, she shares stories of Native women runners from across North America, whether they've run two miles or two hundred. "Oftentimes, Native women are stereotyped in many ways, including overly sexualized through costumes or dehumanized through mascots," Verna added. "I want us to be uplifted in positive ways."

In 2019, she decided to lend her voice to another issue: Missing and Murdered Indigenous Women and Girls (MMIWG)—an ongoing humanitarian crisis in Canada and the United States. In both countries, Native women are murdered at disproportionately high rates. In the United States, Indigenous women are 1.2 times more likely than white women to experience violence over their lifetimes.

A 1978 Supreme Court ruling stripped sovereign tribes of their ability to effectively prosecute non-Native offenders, leaving Native women and girls especially at risk. Even though the 2013 Violence Against Women Reauthorization Act partially restored the criminal jurisdiction of tribal governments, four out of five Native women still experience violence, including sexual violence, physical violence, and stalking—and overwhelmingly by non-Native perpetrators.

In 2019, Verna organized a May 5 run in honor of a grassroots campaign to honor Missing and Murdered

Indigenous Women and Girls. In doing so, she became one of many Indigenous voices calling for the U.S. government to federally recognize May 5 as an official day of awareness. "I had this idea that anyone could run wherever they were so that they could be a part of this movement," Verna explained. A resolution was finally passed in 2021, coinciding with Verna's second virtual run, which yielded 3,500 participants and raised over $86,000 for MMIW USA.

The wife and mother of four has come a long way over the past thirteen years. Her journey from brand-new runner to marathoner to ultrarunner has also been a journey of activism and healing. "Running isn't just a physical activity; there's a lot of healing, ceremony—medicine for our people," said Verna. "Oftentimes, non-Natives don't understand that, but for Natives, running has always been a part of life."

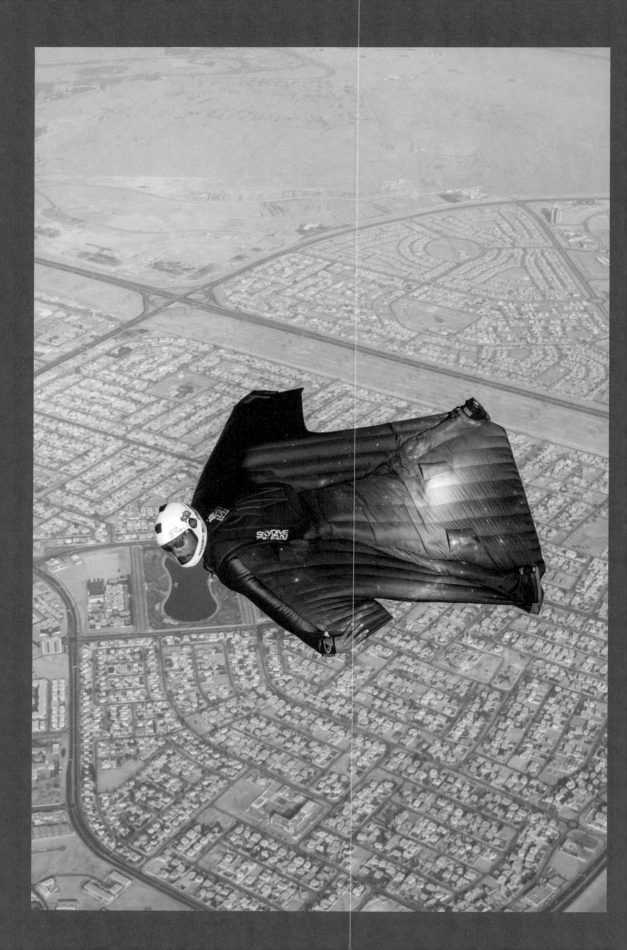

Learning to Fly

featuring Brandon Johnson

DUBAI, UNITED ARAB EMIRATES

BRANDON JOHNSON IS A THIRTY-THREE-YEAR-OLD AFRICAN American professional skydiver with over 9,000 solo jumps. The 6'4" air force veteran began skydiving in 2013 after watching a viral video of Jeb Corliss wingsuit-flying through the Schattenbach canyon in the Swiss Alps.

As soon as he reached the recommended 200 jumps, Brandon learned how to wingsuit. "It's a suit that becomes pressurized when it fills up with air, enabling you to slow down your vertical descent and increase your forward air speed," he explained. "It allows you to cover larger distances and gives you the feeling of actually flying." While he's flown quite a few wingsuits over the years, a crowd favorite is a customized version depicting two different images from the Hubble Space Telescope. "I've got a bit of a fascination with space and decided that I wanted my

wingsuit to reflect that," said Brandon enthusiastically.

He typically spends ten months out of each year working at a drop zone in Dubai and two months working at a drop zone back home in Texas. Life as a professional skydiver means early mornings and late nights and physically demanding work shooting aerial videography, certifying new solo jumpers, and taking tandem students on their very first skydive. One of his most memorable was actor Will Smith and their 2018 tandem skydive over the Palm Jumeirah, a famous tourist attraction in Dubai.

Brandon also did a crash course in BASE jumping in Brento, Italy, with friends. "BASE jumping involves jumping from a fixed object," he explained. "The acronym stands for *building*, *antenna*, *span*, and *earth*. There are no backups, so the risk is a lot higher." His goals have expanded since the early days of dub-step edits and wingsuit BASE videos. Skydiving has so many niche activities like demonstration jumps, vertical formation skydiving, big-way records, and advanced canopy piloting, and he's eager to do them all. He's currently flying a 79-square-foot parachute, which allows him to swoop out of the sky and land at speeds of up to 80 mph.

Thankfully, his family has long since reconciled themselves to his love of sky-diving. "They think I'm crazy, but they appreciate the fact that I'm having fun and living life," said Brandon.

I Would Walk
8,000 Miles . . .

featuring Tyler Lau

LOS ANGELES, CALIFORNIA

CHUMASH, TONGVA KIZH

IN 2018, TYLER LAU HIKED 8,000 MILES ALONG THE CONTINENTAL Divide Trail, the Pacific Crest Trail, and the Appalachian Trail, becoming the first Person of Color and the first Asian American to complete a Calendar Year Triple Crown. He's also the first resident of Hong Kong to do so.

Growing up, Tyler spent summers in Hong Kong and school years in the United States. After college, he wandered for a bit, working in conservation and studying organic farming in New Zealand before returning to the United States to join trail crews all over the country. He even moved to Montana for a season of wildland firefighting before returning to Southern California.

Even before he set out to accomplish the impossible, the former distance runner had long been enamored with seeing the world on foot. He was drawn to hiking as a good way to slow down and see the world at its own pace. "I like the simplicity of using my body to get places," said Tyler.

Tyler is an interesting combination of romantic and realist. He fondly recalls in one breath "being out there without reception, walking and trying to find the essentials—water and a place to sleep." In the next, he describes "trying to get to the next town to honestly find a place to poop where you're not going to get eaten alive by mosquitos."

In 2016, two years before his successful Calendar Year Triple Crown, Tyler set out on his first long-distance hike along the Pacific Crest Trail. It's a 2,653-mile route that begins in British Columbia at the United States/Canada border and passes through ten mountain ranges and seven national parks before reaching its terminus along the United States/Mexico border. It was a humbling experience. He set out on the trail with an overweight pack, got one of the biggest blisters of his life, and spent the next three days recovering. Tyler didn't give up, though, and not long after set his sights on the Calendar Year Triple Crown—no easy feat. In 2018, only four people had completed all three long-distance hikes in under twelve months, and they were all white men.

So how did he prepare for the hike?

Tyler moved home and saved every penny he could for thirteen months. "I took every extra job or side gig I could find—even if it was just $30," Tyler recalled. "That was another resupply box or hostel stay. You start attaching numbers to things." In total, he saved $16,500, most of which was spent on food. He bought protein bars in bulk, mostly the same two flavors. "You do get sick of them, but you just eat it and keep going," he added. "I got to the point where food was just calories."

In addition to protein bars, he ate processed foods: cookies, crackers, chips, and even cold-soaked instant mashed potatoes. They were lighter and packed smaller than fresh fruits and vegetables. The irony wasn't lost on him. "I was eating like that by choice but I realize that some people don't have any other options," Tyler reflected.

Apart from food, clothing and gear was also a concern. During the nine-month trek, Tyler went through sixteen pairs of shoes and ten pairs of socks while hiking an average of thirty to thirty-five miles each day. On the western trails, his personal record was fifty-two miles in a single day—the equivalent of two back-to-back marathons. To pass the time, he listened to music and podcasts and tried to stay out of his head. The Appalachian Trail was another story.

The third and final leg of the Calendar Year Triple Crown occurred during the wettest year on record. He got caught in an early snow in Pennsylvania. "That was really tough having to break trail on your own every day," said Tyler. "I don't think I was ever dry." There were many times when he felt ready to call it quits. "I used to call people when I had reception," Tyler admitted. "I just wanted to say to someone that I was ready to be done. Luckily no one picked up."

After taking a few days off to recover from an injury, Tyler felt better and was able to push on. After all, finishing strong wasn't just about him. During the hike, he fundraised over $8,000 for organizations supporting diversity and equity in the outdoors and getting youth outside. He also helped raise funds for a cousin who was hospitalized in a coma after a tragic accident.

Surprisingly, or maybe unsurprisingly, he's had a mixed reception since becoming the ninth person ever and the first Person of Color to complete a Calendar Year Triple Crown. "It's not really something I bring up," said Tyler. Part of the issue has been dealing with the more toxic elements of hiking culture. Even

before he began his attempt, Tyler dealt with casual racism and microaggressions as an Asian American man in a mostly white community.

As a project leader for trail crews, he had to deal with white people, a mostly older generation, talking down to him. "I found when managing groups you can't respond to every negative comment—kind of like the Internet—or you'll be out of energy," said Tyler. Since completing the Calendar Year Triple Crown, he's dealt with racism online and in person. After a popular outdoor magazine

released a video of footage from his hike, the social media post was flooded with racist comments. "The negative and vitriolic backlash against me simply saying that I'd be the first Person of Color to complete a Calendar Year Triple Crown was really off-putting," Tyler confessed.

At the end of the day, his goal was to show that thru-hiking isn't just for one group.

"If I can show another Asian kid out there that this is something they can pursue and achieve, then that's my purpose," said Tyler.

Breathing Through Fear

featuring Cheyenne Smith

BOULDER, COLORADO

HINONO'EINO (ARAPAHO), TSISTSISTAS (CHEYENNE), NÚUCHI-U (UTE)

"THE FIRST TIME I GOT ON A HIGHLINE, I FELT SO MUCH FEAR," SAID Cheyenne Smith, a twenty-four-year-old climber and slackliner in Boulder, Colorado. Cheyenne began rock scrambling at a young age and picked up slacklining in high school. Slacklining became something she did alone in the park by herself.

She loved how accessible it was. In theory, anyone could buy the $15 webbing and carabiners to rig the line between two trees. In practice, the sport—similar to tightrope walking but more dynamic—appeals mostly to young white men, perhaps owing to the sport's proximity to climbing and BASE jumping.

Then one afternoon at the park, she ran into a few highliners—advanced slackliners who rig their webbing between cliffs.

"It's a really scary thing to be that high off the ground," Cheyenne admitted. "There's a level of resilience involved. You have to keep showing up. It's not going to click the first five or ten times." Learning

meant putting herself out there constantly. She kept showing up to the park looking for other people to highline with. Cheyenne also joined Facebook groups and reached out to total strangers with mixed results.

Eventually she met a mentor, and she learned how to rig and even acquired her own gear. Her goal is to pay it forward by introducing beginners to the sport. For now, progressing means making more mistakes, and learning from them.

The fear isn't gone. It's something she's learned to live with. "You can sit through fear, breathe through it," Cheyenne explained. How many of us spend our weekends facing our fears while balanced 500 feet above ground? Even though highlining has had only one recorded fatality in the past thirty years,

the fear factor alone is enough to keep most people away. There are also many ways to get hurt in the sport, ranging from a sprained ankle while hiking to an injury from improperly rigging, mounting, or dismounting the line.

While she balances on the highline, Cheyenne remains tethered to the webbing by a twelve-foot climbing rope and two aluminum rings. It doesn't prevent her from falling, but it does keep her safe. Each fall into clean air is exponentially safer than the broken bones that could result from climbing her favorite routes in Eldorado Canyon. Even though highlining is technically safer than climbing, the 360-degree exposure tells a different visual story. Nevertheless, "falling reminds me that I am safe," said Cheyenne.

Not Your
Model Minority

featuring Nirvana Ortanez

MOUNT HOOD, OREGON

WATLALA, CONFEDERATED TRIBES OF GRAND RONDE, CONFEDERATED TRIBES OF SILETZ INDIANS

THE WAY NIRVANA ORTANEZ TELLS IT, SOY SAUCE NATION BEGAN AT A snowboarding camp in Mount Hood, Oregon. She was in a room with fellow counselors when one guy stood up and introduced himself as "AK, short for Andrew Kelly—not 'Asian Kid.'" He'd just finished with a joke about how he was used to being "the only Asian" when they both locked eyes. Soon afterward, a friendship was born.

In 2012, they founded Soy Sauce Nation, an affinity group celebrating snowboarders of Asian descent. Recently, Nirvana helped organize the first-ever Soy Sauce Nationals, which drew snowboarders from all over the United States, plus one participant from Japan. The small team of organizers has plans to expand the event and hopefully attract even more snowboarders from across the Asian diaspora.

Nirvana is a thirty-year-old Filipino marketing professional for a large outdoor brand. She's also a former pro snowboarder. She grew up in Mission Beach, San Diego, with her parents and brother. Her family surfed, went snowboarding together, and spent a lot of time outdoors. Nirvana attended mostly white schools in affluent neighborhoods where she and her brother were always one of a handful of Asian kids. In her friend group, she was typically the only one. "When I was younger, I didn't realize that I was any different," Nirvana recollected.

She was fifteen or sixteen and had just won a snowboarding competition when her dad told her that sponsorships would be difficult for her to obtain because she wasn't blonde or white. "I remember him saying that it would be really hard to get paid to do this professionally because I wasn't considered to be marketable," Nirvana recalled.

"At that time, my reaction was 'no, you don't know anything,'" said Nirvana, but the conversation stuck with her. Looking back, she now understands that he was warning her of the sort of obstacles that lay ahead. Much later, she experienced the discrimination he had alluded to while competing at a World Cup for the opportunity to represent the Philippines in the 2014 Sochi Olympics. The experience was far from what she had expected. She remembers not being taken seriously by the other competitors. "They paint this sense of unity and camaraderie within sports that just wasn't present," said Nirvana. However, her determination to become a professional snowboarder meant overlooking discrimination in a sport that is far from diverse.

Then she met Andrew Kelly. "Meeting AK and realizing that there are people who look like us—and seeing them all together—was an awakening," Nirvana explained. Part of the experience has also been finding out just how many shared experiences they have in common. For members, that has included swapping stories about being a transracial adoptee, or the only "Asian kid" in their group of friends, or the "only Asian snowboarder" they know. It also caused

her to realize that "unless you have parents or a friend introducing you to snowboarding—or other extreme sports—there are significant barriers to entry."

In the past ten years, Soy Sauce Nation has been a public declaration of racial pride, friendship, and community building around a shared identity. While Asian pro snowboarders like Chloe Kim, Hailey Langland, and Miles Fallon have grabbed headlines and titles in recent years, the sport remains very white. Recent headlines of anti-Asian violence and hate crimes have also reinforced the need for safe spaces like Soy Sauce Nation. "Sometimes I feel super helpless," Nirvana admitted. "The whole stereotype of Asians being polite or keeping their head down—those are things I've done. I feel, especially with Soy Sauce Nation and snowboarding, it's like, no, I don't want to be quiet about those things anymore." Soy Sauce Nation not only is empowering, but it has also helped evolve her perspective as a minority within the sport. "I understand now that people need other people who look like them to think that they can succeed in a space," said Nirvana.

While working hard to provide an affinity space for other snowboarders of Asian descent, Nirvana was also experiencing her own identity crisis—not around race, but around her future as a snowboarder. She watched her friends slowly leave the sport due to injury, career changes, or relationships pulling them in different directions. "I felt super lost for a second," she admitted. For someone who had always valued snowboarding as a source of community, the change was difficult and it left her feeling empty.

During that time, she was also coaching and filming "video parts" for additional

income. "It's a niche in action sports," said Nirvana, "You find a feature—a downrail or handrail—and you build your own spot, to include the ramp and landing. It has to be during winter and there must be snow." Filming rail tricks was physically and mentally exhausting and the money wasn't enough. "That was a big blow to my ego and a stopping point," said Nirvana. "If I'm maxing out what I can give to snowboarding, why should I keep going?"

So she stopped. After six years of working as a pro snowboarder, she decided to pursue a different path. Recently she's gone through other changes, including marrying her longtime partner and moving back to California, where they live close enough to the beach to surf in the morning and ride their bikes. "Surfing was my first sport," said Nirvana. "I'm really excited to fall in love with it again." She also has big plans to hit the slopes this winter, and maybe visit summer snowboarding camps in Chile or New Zealand in the near future. Snowboarding is still a big part of her life. "For me, it's about lifelong friends and a community I can call home," said Nirvana.

Guide to Outdoor Allyship: Part 2

SELF-AWARENESS

WE ALL EXPERIENCE THE OUTDOORS DIFFERENTLY

When you pass others on the trail, do they smile, meet your eye, or greet you? Don't assume this is a universal experience—it isn't. While many of us enjoy spending time in nature, it often comes at a price, such as stares and unwanted comments about our skin color, queerness, weight, or perceived ability. Sometimes the cost comes in the form of hostile interactions, racial slurs, and traffic stops. This was certainly true for a Black couple scouting for picnic locations in Starkville, Mississippi, where a white Kampgrounds of America employee pulled a gun on them. It was also true for the Black attorney pushing his son in a stroller at a Washington, DC, park who was flagged by police after a white woman reported a "suspicious man walking the bike path with a baby." It's hard to be enthralled by nature when you're worried about your physical safety among crowds of white people who view your dark skin as a threat. Know that your positive experience at the crag or lake or Burning Man is not universal. Anti-Blackness in particular means your Black friends and colleagues may not always feel safe in the outdoors.

ALLIES ARE AWARE OF THEIR OWN PREJUDICE

That's why part two of allyship is to examine your own implicit biases. Increasing your awareness of your own prejudice is an important part of allyship. So is accepting the fact that whiteness insulates you from race-based stress and systemic racism. Do you prefer activities where other white people lead or take up the most space? Do you feel uncomfortable or less safe when your guide is a Black woman? Or when you have to remember to use *they/them* pronouns? Do you lock your car door when you unexpectedly see Black people at the trailhead? Do you feel irritation when a language other than English is spoken? Or when your favorite waterfall from childhood is suddenly packed with selfie-taking *urban* hikers? Do you feel annoyed when the switchbacks are crowded with multigenerational families wearing inexpensive sandals instead of $200 hiking shoes and eating samosas instead of protein bars? What about your online habits? Do you refuse to geo-tag outdoor pics while demanding that new hikers—who are disproportionately Black, Indigenous, and People of Color

(BIPOC)—contribute sweat equity and find it themselves? Do you really want hikers to be safe, well prepared, and well informed, or do you feel a strong sense of personal ownership over public lands that you do not own and that your ancestors did not steward over millennia?

Do you feel uncomfortable having this conversation—even just with yourself? Talking about privilege and prejudice can definitely be discomforting, but if your instinct is to silence conversations about race, ignore it.

IT'S OKAY TO TALK ABOUT RACE

White privilege means you probably didn't grow up talking about race. Maybe you were even taught that the mere acknowledgment of race was, um, racist, right? Even though you're now an adult, you sometimes still hide behind statements like "I don't see color" or "nature is color-blind." The end result is that you benefit from racism (and ableism) while also silencing People of Color who try to talk about discrimination. Do you struggle to understand why your Black and brown colleagues are uncomfortable around white people who stare at them when they wear their hair as it naturally grows from their head or speak their heritage language? We're also being a little dramatic when we talk about triggers or

the need for safe spaces, right? Do you feel annoyed at our "political posts" and "overly emotional" responses on social media regarding the lack of public outcry over missing and murdered Indigenous women or recent violent attacks against Asian people? Maybe you like Native-inspired fashion or K-pop. Obviously, that doesn't mean you have to get upset when Native and Asian people living in the United States are systematically targeted and discriminated against, right? It's not like we're family or anything. Or maybe you do have close friends or family who identify as BIPOC. In that case, there's something else you should know. Proximity to People of Color doesn't make you anti-racist.

PROXIMITY TO PEOPLE OF COLOR DOESN'T MAKE YOU AN ALLY

Don't use your partner, friends, kids, or relatives to demonstrate that you are not racist. We love you, but our existence is not meant to shield you from accountability or self-awareness. Proximity to People of Color doesn't mean that you don't say or do racist things. More importantly, it's important to understand that racism is a hierarchy-based system of power that confers unearned advantages to some based solely on the color of their skin

while disenfranchising, criminalizing, and dehumanizing others, based solely on the color of their skin. There's no way to individually opt out without dismantling the entire system. If someone is bringing a problematic statement or behavior to your attention, do some self-reflection before you deflect with "my employee/friend/partner/child is Black; therefore I can't be racist."

SOMETIMES IT'S HARD FOR US TO TALK TO YOU ABOUT RACISM

Are you a white, cisgender, heterosexual male? If you have friends whose identities aren't identical to your own, it's highly possible that their experience in the outdoors may not mirror yours. It's also possible that, if you asked them if they've ever been discriminated against, their answer might still be no. Why is that? Are we purposefully misleading you? Even though our competence and presence in the outdoors are more likely to be questioned than yours, even though we are less likely to see people who look like us on the trail, even though our mistakes are more likely to be misattributed to our race or gender, we—your friends, partner, or family who identify as People of Color—may not want to talk to you about racism. Yep, it's complicated.

Why wouldn't we be 100 percent honest with you? Sometimes the decision is a subconscious one. As we move through the world, People of Color often adjust our behavior, code-switch our language, and guard our thoughts and opinions to keep white people comfortable.

I do this all the time without thinking: I switch to my telephone voice, add ma'am/sir, and drop Black colloquial expressions. I change my inflection, and, most importantly, I smile so white people don't perceive me as threatening. This has never been truer than while hiking alone in state and national parks, where I am often the only Black face on the trail. I even move off the path, out of habit, to let white people pass, despite being visibly disabled and using mobility aids. But we're not always code-switching to keep you comfortable! Sometimes we just aren't self-aware, or we have other forms of privilege that protect us from the worst forms of racism. And sometimes we consciously choose not to. It's possible that you are not (yet) ready for a discussion on race and privilege. Your knee-jerk response is still #notallwhitepeople. Or you want to "love and light" racism away without acknowledging that it exists or that you benefit from it. Even though you know the definition of racism, you still cling to the idea that being a nice person is enough. So, you gaslight us and tone-police our responses to racism, and we eventually stop sharing.

Vehicles Are Not Required

featuring Ananth Maniam

SEATTLE, WASHINGTON

COAST SALISH, STILLAGUAMISH, DUWAMISH, MUCKLESHOOT, SUQUAMISH

"MOST PEOPLE GO TO THE MOUNTAINS FOR SOLITUDE," SAID ANANTH Maniam, a thirty-one-year-old mountaineer living in Seattle, Washington. "I think the reason why I return over and over again has to do with my search for identity and community." Ananth is best known for completing 450+ ascents in his first four and a half years of living in the Pacific Northwest—most without owning a car. You can find him outdoors, guiding backcountry trips and sometimes completing multiple ascents in a single week. "It depended on bus availability," said Ananth.

Surprisingly, he didn't grow up in the mountains. Ananth grew up in Chennai, India, where he spent most of his school vacations on his grandfather's farm, harvesting coconut and sugarcane. From a young age, he dreamed of going to the mountains one day. As a teenager, Ananth and a friend traveled around his home state of Tamil Nadu. "Traveling by bus around my state where everyone speaks the same language was good preparation for what came next," said

Ananth. After graduating from an engineering college, he saved half of his income for two years to fund a trek to the Himalayas.

The experience was eye-opening. There were breathtaking alpine vistas and glacier crossings, but there was also the struggle of communicating in a foreign language. "When I went to Kashmir, communication was a challenge because I didn't speak any Hindi," Ananth recalled. "Even though we looked the same, we all spoke different languages. I spent most of that trip entirely out of my comfort zone." He kept his phone charged so each evening he could emotionally recharge by listening to music in his mother tongue, Tamil, one of India's 447 languages.

In 2016, he immigrated to the United States. Ananth did a lot of research prior to his arrival in Seattle and set his sights on mountaineering as a way to make friends and integrate into the local community. There was only one problem: he didn't own a vehicle. "Most of the trips required a car, or had a fee associated, or you had to know people," said Ananth, referring to local climbing organizations. Those barriers made it difficult for a beginner like himself to get outdoors.

After weighing his options, he joined the Seattle Transit Hikers. "There was no car requirement and the concept was simple," Ananth said. "You take public transportation—a bus or train—from where you live to the trailhead."

Today, part of his mission as an experienced mountaineer is to show that public transportation can be a viable option for people looking to get outside and explore local trails. It's not a perfect solution, but it does make the outdoors more accessible for individuals who don't have access to a vehicle.

Upon his arrival in Seattle, he was struck by the difference between public transportation in India, which is heavily invested in, and the United States. "It's more difficult here," said Ananth. "If I have a car, I can get to the trailhead in thirty minutes. If I don't have a car, it may take three and a half hours."

In 2017, Ananth, alongside other outdoor communities, began working with Seattle Department of Transportation to improve transportation to the city's many local trails. The end result was a new service called Trailhead Direct. It provides round trips from the city center to trailheads around Seattle and can be accessed using a city pass. It also runs every thirty minutes.

Transportation isn't the only barrier to access for many People of Color. "In the Himalayas, we carried really heavy gear that was a lot cheaper than what I've come across here," said Ananth. "The gear we have in the U.S. is lighter but way too expensive." While he's pushed for affordable transportation to Seattle-area trailheads, he's also supportive of efforts across the United States to decrease barriers to entry by promoting affordable gear through lending libraries, secondhand gear markets, gear maintenance, and more. "Similar to racial equity, socioeconomic equity is really important," said Ananth.

To date, Ananth has completed over 450 ascents. However, he didn't start out climbing mountains. Ananth initially began hiking accessible trails with lower elevation gain. Next, he took a few courses with a local club called The Mountaineers, which enhanced his knowledge of scrambling, rock climbing, and glacier climbing.

At the time, he noticed there weren't that many People of Color leading trips. "That's one thing I wanted to change," said Ananth, who worked his way up from novice to trip leader.

Today he guides advanced trips in remote areas. He's been leading trips for three and a half years. In 2019, he earned the "Mountaineers Leader of the Year" award, the first immigrant and the youngest person to get the award. While the overall experience has been incredibly rewarding, it includes dealing with microaggressions as the only Person of Color in a group. Oftentimes it's in the form of climbers making assumptions about his technical skills solely based on his physical appearance. "When the microaggressions escalate to efforts to undermine my skills or leadership, it becomes a safety issue," Ananth added. This is a longstanding issue that he feels mountaineering organizations can, and must, do more to address.

"Most of the time I ignore it," Ananth confessed. However, there are times when he addresses fear-based microaggressions on the spot before they impact morale. "When someone says, 'I don't trust where you're going. I want to go another way,' we always pull together and have a group discussion," said Ananth. "I ask them to take out their map and tell me where they are. They might just be scared and in need of reassurance." In the moment, his job is to stay calm and level-headed. "At the end of the day, it's not about me as an individual or the person doing the microaggression; it's about safety," he added. That doesn't mean that being judged by his skin color versus his ability doesn't bother him. It does.

Despite the barriers he's faced along the way, Ananth remains committed to making mountaineering and the outdoors community more accessible to people of all racial, ethnic, and socio-economic backgrounds. For now, his home remains in the mountains. "As a first-generation immigrant living in the U.S. 9,000 miles away from home, the people I find in the outdoors are my family," Ananth explained. "The mountains push me out of my comfort zone and that really appeals to me."

Pedal 2 the People

featuring Dr. Rachel Olzer

MINNEAPOLIS, MINNESOTA
WAHPEKUTE, OČHÉTHI ŠAKÓWIŊ

DR. RACHEL OLZER IS A QUEER BLACK CYCLIST AND THE EXECUTIVE director of an outdoors nonprofit. Over the past few years, she's completed a PhD in evolutionary biology, co-founded an online affinity space for cyclists of Color, and written for major publications about her experience as an African American mountain biker.

Although she now calls Bentonville, Arkansas, home, Rachel grew up in Las Vegas, Nevada. "I didn't find out that I was adopted until I was twelve, which is when I first realized that I was not white," she recalled. "I didn't even learn about the words *transracial adoptee* until I met other people—particularly in cycling—whose stories really helped me put the pieces together."

The sponsored athlete began riding in high school. In college, she purchased a mountain bike to access a local climbing area. It was there that another climber openly mocked her in front of others. "I came down and immediately started crying," Rachel recalled. "After that, I didn't really want to climb anymore. I focused on biking, getting really strong, and finding joy in that."

For Rachel, the incident epitomized the widespread elitism and racial prejudice in the climbing community and helped jumpstart her search for community outside of it.

After college, she moved to Minnesota to attend graduate school. "I was nervous because I knew it was going to be a huge change," said Rachel. "It was my first time leaving the Southwest, where adventure is right in your face." At the same time, she was excited about Minneapolis's robust cycling community and infrastructure. The reality was somewhere in between, however. People stared a lot, making her even more acutely aware of being the only Person of Color in many social, academic, and outdoor settings. The racial segregation was also in stark contrast to her childhood in Nevada, where racism felt less in

her face. In Minneapolis, it pervaded university life, where all of the fifty-plus faculty in her department were white and where she was often the only Person of Color at cycling meetups.

To make matters worse, Rachel spent her first Midwest winter struggling with seasonal depression in an apartment that lacked heating. She gradually found herself spending more and more time online in search of community and other cyclists of Color. Eventually, a few of her new mountain biking friends came out to Minneapolis for a visit. "It helped me turn a corner with my relationship to Minnesota and Minneapolis—that I could show them this place that had gorgeous scenery and great riding," she recalled.

Despite all of the challenges that were stacking up, she also enjoyed growing and learning as a mountain biker. Rachel bought a cyclocross bike, which she used for commuting, racing, and bike packing; she did her first overnight trip to Wisconsin's Northwoods to camp and enjoy the fall foliage; and she teamed up with Pedal2thePeople co-founder Eric Arce to publish stories of diverse cyclists online. "Storytelling is super powerful," said Rachel. "Not only were we providing a space for people to tell their stories, but it also had a reciprocal effect." She felt empowered to pen her own story for several major publications, which helped her process her grief after George Floyd's murder by a white Minneapolis police officer challenged the sense of safety and community she had worked so hard to build.

While living in Minnesota, Rachel also befriended other transracial adoptees whose experiences mirrored her own. "Once I started writing about it, I was then connected to even more people," she explained. "It's super healing to know I'm not alone. Having the language to be able to understand and seek out support is so powerful." Part of that healing has meant holding space for her family members whose conservative politics and views on race contradict Rachel's activism. "I have to hold their ability to change close to my heart," she added. "That helps me see their humanity and continue to love them."

Recently she has also focused inward on becoming more vocal with her own needs—especially as a disabled athlete who has lived with lupus her entire life and diabetes the better part of her adult life. That includes resting when she needs it and canceling plans guilt-free. Embracing change and imperfection has also come along with switching up her riding style from cross-country racing to downhill and enduro. Lately, that has included becoming comfortable with starting over as a beginner and making mistakes. "You don't do a PhD for instant gratification." She laughed. "I guess I'm somebody who is okay with sticking things out, but I also think the more you can be okay with the process, the better off you are."

American Traditional Ink

featuring Marina Inoue

RICHMOND, VIRGINIA

POWHATAN

MARINA INOUE IS A BIRACIAL JAPANESE AMERICAN ROCK CLIMBER and former vanlifer. The only child of a graphic designer and freelance still-life photographer, it's perhaps no surprise that she has made a career as a tattoo artist, specializing in American traditional ink.

Growing up in New York City, she wasn't really into athletics. Outside of exploring abandoned urban spaces and tagging, Marina mostly visited museums and art galleries with her parents or spent time alone. "I was never really a sporty kid," she recalled. "I never found anything I connected with physically." It wasn't until Marina moved to Virginia at age twenty-six and accepted an invitation to a local gym that she began sport climbing and bouldering. The experience was transformative.

Climbing became a new way of connecting to her body. "It's an interesting combination of physical strength, mental acuity, and also technical skills," she reflected. "My brain could turn off and I could just feel my body moving." Marina wasn't just figuring out routes and bouldering problems; she was

experiencing *flow state*—a term coined by Hungarian American psychologist Mihaly Csikszentmihalyi that has been used in connection with everyone from artists to athletes.

"I'm a little grateful I started climbing as a grown-up even though my body hurts," she added. Perhaps because she missed out on youth climbing leagues and competitive sports entirely, she's developed her own unique approach toward climbing. "My only competition is myself," she admitted. "I really like to climb things that are powerful and that make me feel powerful. I enjoy dynamic movement, jumping, and steep angles with bigger holds." Her favorite places to climb include Rifle, Colorado, where she climbed Tomb Raider, her first 5.13d, and the New River Gorge.

One thing she likes about working on challenging routes is pushing through her initial nervousness and anxiety. "The fear is so intense at first," said Marina. "There are a lot of unknowns. I don't know if it's going to be too hard for me; I don't know what the hold is like; I don't know what falling will be like."

Lately, her journey has included educating herself about who has access to outdoor spaces and who doesn't. Viewing climbing culture through a more critical lens means reexamining a lot of what she accepted or took for granted as a new climber.

"I've gone through growing pains, especially in the last few years," said Marina. "I find myself simultaneously rejecting climbing culture while also deeply embracing a smaller community." It has influenced *where* she's willing to climb and *with whom*. If it means limiting her circle to individuals who are also willing to deconstruct their own privilege and take an active stance against capitalism, racism, queerphobia, transphobia, and ableism, so be it.

She's spent the past year supporting mutual aid efforts and helping set up a climbing mentorship program for marginalized communities. "I'm not white, but my proximity is very, very close," Marina reflected, which has sometimes made her reluctant to personally participate in affinity spaces for fear of denying space to more marginalized people. At the same time, she's also seeking out other climbers of Color. "There's a shared experience with East Asian climbers of being othered in the United States," Marina added. "To be able to climb without having to explain myself, or be on edge, is really important."

I Could Help People Feel Safe

featuring Jalen Bazile

GOLDEN, COLORADO

TSISTSISTAS (CHEYENNE), NÚUCHI-U (UTE)

JALEN BAZILE IS A TWENTY-EIGHT-YEAR-OLD BIRACIAL MOUNTAIN biker living in Golden, Colorado, at the base of the Rocky Mountains. He grew up on Karankawa and Atakapa land in a diverse suburb of Houston, Texas, the nation's fourth most populous city. "I was one of those don't-come-home-until-the-streetlights-come-on kind of kids," said Jalen. His dad bought him a bike when he was four years old and he learned how to ride within a week, spending hours at the park across the street. Jalen began cycling to school as a teenager and continued every chance he could during college.

After his freshman year, he moved cross-country to a small unincorporated town in Colorado, where he worked as a summer camp counselor. It fulfilled a childhood dream of living in a log cabin one day. "I didn't know anything about the mountains, but I came back the following year and never left," Jalen recalled. Groceries were an hour's drive away. The remote location appealed to him, as did the tight-knit community of mostly white skiers, rock climbers, and backpackers

who served as camp instructors. He had discovered a sanctuary from city life, a place where he could be himself and pursue his passion.

Jalen began exploring the dirt and gravel roads around the property on his bike. Mountain biking became a way for the Houston transplant to build a connection with the land. He quickly became known as the guy who rode his bike year-round in all types of weather. "I was always pretty willing to go do stuff on my own," Jalen explained. "Even if I didn't have a community around me, I'd just do it by myself." The commitment paid off later on, when he began leading mountain biking trips.

In 2017, Jalen booked a one-way ticket to Banff, Alberta, in Canada and biked 1,800 miles south along the Great

Divide, the longest unpaved mountain biking route in the world. The solo trip felt empowering. "When I set out, I was asking myself, what am I capable of?" Jalen reflected. "I knew I definitely wanted to do it again, although maybe next time, I wouldn't pay for it on a credit card." Two months later, he quit his job as a camp instructor to ride across the entire Baja Peninsula—another 1,800-mile ride. The once-in-a-lifetime bikepacking trips gave him a sense of adventure and an unexpected feeling: loneliness.

"Yes, I was meeting people, but having such a life-altering experience, and not having anybody back home to share that experience with was challenging," Jalen confessed. "I was really struggling with this on both rides."

His experience mirrors that of many Black, Indigenous, and People of Color who sometimes feel alienated from the communities they grew up in or the mostly white adventure sports that they enjoy on the weekends or both. For many of us, it's also more complex than just race. Our families back home may not be able to afford thousand-dollar bikes, or the outdoor experiences we're passionate about may simply seem unrelatable to them—or may seem like unnecessary risks.

For Jalen, the biggest challenge was not having access to a community of fellow Black mountain bikers. That led him to move to Denver, where he began working in a climbing gym and leading trips with Outdoor Afro. He eventually became a founding member of the Black Foxes, a Black international cycling collective. He had always believed that pursuing his passion would allow him to attract a community of like-minded people. Moving into a more diverse urban area wasn't giving up on his childhood dream. It was trading in aesthetics at 8,600 feet for a chance to build the community he had long been searching for—from the ground up in a mile-high city.

"The Black Foxes aim to rewrite our narrative within outdoor spaces," Jalen explained. "I think being a part of the Black Foxes provides me the opportunity to sit at tables that I wouldn't otherwise be able to sit at and provide advocacy and representation."

Recently, Jalen has been rewriting his own story within the sport. That includes giving a lot of thought to the balance between community and athletic pursuits in his personal life. "I love how amazing mountain biking is," he reflected. "I really like the connection to the land. I think what's more important is sharing this versus doing it solo." Since biking a total of 3,600 miles across North America, he hasn't planned a single long-distance solo trip. "Camaraderie, mentorship, and community are way more important than any single objective," he added.

He recently helped lead a Black Foxes bikepacking trip in the Blue Ridge Mountains. "Because of my experience, I could help people feel safe," said Jalen. "I had a lot of solo time early on; now it's time to really give back because I want to see myself and other people out there." His lifelong dream is to help other People of Color thrive in the outdoors.

Helping Black Families Thrive in Nature

featuring Zenovia Stephens

HUNTSVILLE, ALABAMA

TSALAGI (CHEROKEE, EAST), SHAWANWAKI/SHAWNEE, S'ATSOYAHA (YUCHI), CHIKASHSHA (CHICKASAW)

ZENOVIA STEPHENS IS A THIRTY-SEVEN-YEAR-OLD WIFE AND MOTHER of three. She's also the co-founder of #BlackHikersWeek and the powerhouse behind Black Kids Adventures, Inc., a nonprofit that introduces Black families to the outdoors.

Zenovia grew up in Chicago, Illinois, and fished a lot with her mom and stepfather on Lake Michigan and during trips to Kentucky and Tennessee. There was even a sleepaway camp she went to at age twelve that involved canoeing, camping, and bonfires. "My journey didn't continue after camp," said Zenovia. "I always had this image that I had to move to Colorado if I wanted to live an adventurous, outdoorsy lifestyle."

Instead, she moved to Alabama to attend college on both track and academic scholarships. It's where the Chicagoan met her now husband. It's also where she fell in love with Alabama's rolling hills and mountains. After dropping out of a chiropractic program, Zenovia dealt with what she now believes was depression and feelings of restlessness. To cope, she began riding her bike on a local greenway. That led to daily hikes on a nearby trail. "I began going there every day to talk to God and find peace," she recalled. "That was the beginning of my hiking journey."

In 2015, when she was pregnant with her second child, Zenovia and her husband decided to stop at DeSoto Falls, a state park in North Alabama on Tsalagi (Cherokee, East) and S'atsoyaha (Yuchi) land. At that moment, with the Little River thundering a hundred feet into the canyon below, she made a decision. "I turned to my husband and said, 'I want to explore all of Alabama,'" she recalled. "Since then, we've been hiking our way across the state and exploring all of the beauty and nature here, which is massive."

Over the past six years, the family of five has traveled to state parks, waterfalls, lakes, and rivers across the state, motivated by a sense of wonder but also by Zenovia's desire to teach her sons and encourage other Black families to explore their own backyard. Initially, living an adventurous lifestyle involved planning around which grandparents could keep the kids in Chicago or Atlanta. "At some point, it occurred to me that I was doing them a disservice by not including them," said Zenovia. "If I didn't discover what was around me until well into adulthood, the same thing could happen to my kids."

Her new goal became to expose her children to as many outdoor activities as possible. These days, the boys hike, camp, and paddle alongside their parents. "White people bring their kids to everything," Zenovia added. "I want my kids to know that this isn't a special vacation activity. You can do this on any given

day." She didn't want them to grow up thinking of the outdoors as a far-off, out-of-reach place. Now she's on a mission to make sure that Black families across the state find their place in the outdoors.

Black Kids Adventures began in the middle of the pandemic. "Our primary goal is to create opportunities for families to get outside and to remove some of the fear that comes from doing these things alone," said Zenovia. She has a lot of empathy for Black people who may be interested in the outdoors but are hesitant to try new things without the support of family, friends, or at least a familiar face. The nonprofit currently hosts two camp-outs a year in rural Alabama, with cabins, hiking, kayaking, canoeing, environmental education programs, and even a taste of farm life. The camp is completely free for attendees, thanks to Zenovia's tireless fundraising efforts to cover the $200 cost per participant. "I wanted it to be free because it's about exposure," she explained. "A lot of times, people won't put their money into things they don't see value in. If I can get you there, you'll see it."

Another part of her mission is to break down common fears and misconceptions about the outdoors in a safe, culturally affirming space where people who are "new to the outdoors" can learn together without fear of judgment. "I've had people who are terrified of bugs, who have no relationship with the outdoors, who have passed on their fear to their children, and I've seen them all flourish," said Zenovia. She is helping Black families create outdoor memories as a community.

Thanks to crowdfunding, grants, and support from people who believe in the mission, Black Kids Adventures has been able to offer additional programming such as themed hikes, a yoga in the park series, and most recently, a stand-up paddle day for local families. She's also making plans to organize a gear closet in the near future. "I'm working from camp to camp, praying and looking for opportunities," said Zenovia. "My goal is to eventually have multiyear funding so I'm not so overwhelmed."

Her advice to families is to start where you are. "Don't let someone else's image of what it means to be outdoorsy pressure you into buying a bunch of gear," Zenovia warned. Her family didn't even purchase hiking boots until they started posting photos on social media where pressure to perform outdoor recreation in a certain way and at a certain price point is admittedly high—but so is the sense of community.

After observing the social impact of #BlackBirdersWeek, a social media campaign created in response to the harassment of an African American Central Park birder in May 2020, Zenovia was inspired to launch #BlackHikersWeek. She reached out to Debbie Njai of Black People Who Hike and Nailah Blades of Color Outside for help with designing the six-day campaign, which includes a daily hashtag and prompt encouraging participants to share photos and connect with other people in the community. The annual event also spotlights many of the leaders within the Black hiking community who are advocating for social change. It has been a welcome change from the one-sided tone that is so often used by the media to reference Black people in the outdoors—that of a deficit or missing demographic, with scarce acknowledgment of existing Black outdoor culture.

Through her work as an industry change-maker and tireless advocate,

Zenovia has never lost sight of her initial goal. "I used to think that hiking meant summiting the highest mountain," said Zenovia. "I want people to know that they belong in these spaces so that they won't feel intimidated to get outdoors."

The Only Black Backpacker on the Trail

featuring Mardi Fuller

BOSTON, MASSACHUSETTS

PAWTUCKET, MASSA-ADCHU-ES-ET (MASSACHUSETT)

MARDI FULLER HAS SPENT THE PAST TWENTY-FOUR YEARS BACKPACK-ing and paddling her way across the Northeast United States. While her favorite moments in the outdoors have included a few destination trips, like the thirty-three-mile Chilkoot Trail from Alaska to British Columbia or the ninety-eight-mile Allagash Wilderness Waterway in Maine, her heart belongs to Wobanadenok, or the White Mountains of New Hampshire. The forty-three-year-old backpacker and trip leader has hiked all forty-eight of its four-thousand-foot peaks.

"The White Mountains are within driving distance of 70 million people," said Mardi. "People come from as far north as Quebec or as far south as New Jersey. They're very popular but can also be dangerous." The highest summit, Agiocochook or Mount Washington, receives nearly 280,000 visitors annually. "Mount Washington seems manageable but it actually has really bad weather and, until recently, the highest wind speed ever recorded in the world (231 mph)," she cautioned.

Her love of hiking began at home. "The culture of calling a walk 'a hike' wasn't something my parents were familiar with, but they loved being outside," she recalled. The outdoors was a diverse space during her early childhood in Westchester County, New York. She grew up among other Black and brown families, learned to swim at the community pool, and went to a summer camp where she fished and paddled with other first-generation Jamaican American kids. It wasn't until her family moved farther upstate to a mostly white suburb that she began to feel a sense of alienation that persisted throughout her young adult years. "I don't think my parents understood the complexities of it," Mardi considered. "They just thought they were giving my brother and I a better education and more opportunities."

The summer before her first year of college, Mardi signed up for a four-day freshman orientation backpacking trip to Vermont's Green Mountains. "I opened up the L.L.Bean catalog, called them, and ordered a backpack, a Therm-a-Rest, and hiking boots," she laughed. "It was so much fun, and I loved it." In 2001, Mardi moved to Boston, where she first heard about the White Mountains. She purchased a guidebook and hiked all forty-eight peaks over the next five years. In 2005, she joined the Appalachian Mountain Club and added winter hiking to her skill set. Her sense of adventure pushed her to try new things, even though being the only Black backpacker on the trail was often challenging. Still, the reward was feeling like she was exactly where she belonged. "I feel as if I'm a part of nature," she explained. "It's

being inside that feels incongruous to me." Moving her body is how she relaxes and feels present in the outdoors. It's also a way for her to process her thoughts—especially as she gets older and life gets more complicated due to tragedy and circumstance.

The outdoor community has also changed over the years. When she first began backpacking, she was frequently the only Black woman in her group of friends. Lately, Mardi has connected with other Black outdoors people thanks to Outdoor Afro, a not-for-profit organization that hosts meetups in fifty-six cities across the United States. "They've pushed me to always look for erased history, for Black and Indigenous stories that haven't been told," said Mardi. Joining a national community of Black naturalists has also helped her add more mindful outdoor practices like nature walks and identifying local plant species.

Mardi's journey from first-time hiker to experienced trip leader has also been its own reward. "I love being able to stand on top of a mountain, look in a different direction, and recognize a ridgeline," she reflected. "It makes me feel self-confident and accomplished." She hikes for the fresh air, the 360-degree summit views, and the quiet moments on the trail, but her biggest sense of accomplishment comes from introducing newer hikers to the backcountry. There are so many factors that go into organizing a successful hike, from route finding to planning around extreme weather. "Mastering all of those things and being able to craft an enjoyable experience for someone else is a challenge," said Mardi. "I'm proud of how far I've come."

Lesser-Known Waterways

featuring Adam Edwards

PORTLAND, OREGON

STL'PULMSH (COWLITZ), CONFEDERATED TRIBES OF GRAND RONDE, CLACKAMAS, CONFEDERATED TRIBES OF SILETZ INDIANS

THE LAST TIME PROFESSIONAL KAYAKER ADAM EDWARDS NEARLY hiked off river was on the Olympic peninsula in western Washington. Six inches of rain were about to fall, and he and his friends were worried about getting stuck in a box canyon during a flash flood. The alternative—scaling vertical cliffs and hiking miles through dense old-growth forest under heavy rainfall—also sounded dangerous. Ultimately, they decided they could beat the weather and avoid turning a high-risk adventure into something exponentially more serious.

Adam has spent more than a decade chasing historic snowpack, rainstorms, and dam releases in the Pacific Northwest as a member of its tight-knit paddling community. After growing up in a first-generation Caribbean household, he chose Portland because of its proximity to challenging rapids. "Some of my favorite runs, I can do door-to-door in four hours," said Adam. "Two hours on the river and two hours round trip." That's close enough for the full-time arborist to paddle with friends after work or check water levels and select a creek or river to run on the weekends.

Portland offers a range of roadside whitewater, including high-volume options after big snow events and steep creeking—a high-risk technique that involves running low-volume, steep features in a specialized kayak. While local drainages are convenient for after-work adventures, Adam's favorite type of paddling is exploring lesser-known waterways within a few hours of the city. "Exploratory whitewater basically involves paddling a creek or river that either hasn't been run in a decade or two or that is logistically challenging," he clarified.

Part of the appeal is the sheer amount of work that goes into each trip, from map reading to planning on paper to scouting on foot. "If it's really unknown, we usually hike in during late summer when water levels are super low and canyoneer the section to make sure it's doable," Adam explained. The payoff is the opportunity to immerse himself in beautiful natural settings. Adam and his friends' annual fifty-mile paddle on the nearby Sandy River is one example. "We've been trying to go higher and higher up the mountain each summer before we commit to hiking our kayaks through several feet of snow come winter," said Adam.

After losing motivation a few years ago, he slowly started getting back into exploratory whitewater. "I can choose what I paddle and I'm not complacent because I haven't run it already," Adam pointed out. Expedition kayaking, or multiday trips, has played a similar role in allowing him to reconnect with what first drew him to the sport—a desire for adventure, a sense of community and curiosity about the physical world around him. It's taken him to even more locations.

One such trip was a once-in-a-lifetime paddle along the Selway River. The group started out in the mountains of Montana before paddling through the Bitterroot Wilderness into Idaho. "It's Nez Perce land and it's very, very pretty–super expansive with deer, elk, and salmon," Adam described. "You're in the middle of nowhere and then you suddenly pass a multimillion-dollar luxury home with a Cessna parked out front." The remoteness, minus an opulent vacation home or two, was a big part of the experience. He and his friends carried several days of food with them, which meant flipping their boats wasn't an option. They slept out in the open, cooked over open fires, and relied on satellite phones in case of an emergency.

That was a rare summer trip given that kayaking is mostly a winter sport in the Pacific Northwest. "Winter is high-water season while spring and early summer bring snow melt and dam releases," Adam explained. By late summer, low water makes nearby creeks and rivers nearly impassable.

Winter conditions require their own brand of mental toughness and preparation. Kayaking often means hiking miles along old logging trails in freezing temperatures while carrying a sixty-five-pound boat and occasionally swimming out of a challenging hydraulic into bone-chilling water. For safety reasons, Adam carries the same gear regardless of whether or not the whitewater is roadside, exploratory, or expeditionary. He wears a dry suit year-round and a helmet to protect against dangers on the river like partially submerged logs, sharp ledges, and storm debris. He also carries carabiners and throw bags containing

a durable, lightweight rope—ideal for retrieving capsized kayakers and dislodging paddlers who become trapped underwater in their boats. It's also useful for rappelling—a required skill for kayakers operating in the backcountry.

"One of the hardest things when we're doing exploratory or running difficult whitewater is deciding what we're actually going to paddle and what we're going to walk around," said Adam. Walking around an obstacle on the river is known as portaging. Sometimes the entire group will carry their kayaks around a rapid if it can't be safely run.

Or, one individual might rappel down a cliff in order to act as a safety for the other kayakers. In more remote areas in the Pacific Northwest, paddlers like Adam have to budget a portion of their scarce winter daylight hours for scouting rapids, rappelling, portaging, and making on-the-spot safety decisions. On top of that, communication and group dynamics take time.

"When I'm in my boat and paddle up to the lip of a five-foot uniform ledge with the perfect ninety-degree drop and a uniform hydraulic below, that's one thing," said Adam. "However, if it

continues for a football field and it's just ledge after ledge after ledge, I'm going to get out, walk along the bank, and take mental notes." Those quick assessments are the basis of the alpha-beta system that is integral to the functioning of small crews. "One person will hop out, look at the rapid, and decide whether it's an alpha or beta," Adam described. "If it's an alpha, everyone needs to get out and decide if they want to run the rapid. If it's a beta, I might go back and tell the guys, 'You don't need to get out, it's 'middle, middle, left, middle.'" This technique helps them save time on difficult runs, but it requires a lot of trust and collaboration.

Adam credits good friends and exploratory kayaking for propelling his personal growth over the years. "I was the dude bro that paddled hard stuff," said Adam. "Then I was the friendly instructor dude bro that paddled hard stuff. Now I want to share what I can with the local community." He blogs regularly about diversity in the outdoors for Melanin Base Camp and has partnered with Diversify Whitewater to help facilitate beginner-friendly events. Meanwhile, his core group of kayaking friends has grown in more ways than one. "These days, there's a lot more self-awareness and a solid amount of peer-to-peer support," said Adam. "It's not just about challenging ourselves physically anymore; somehow, kayaking has become a vehicle for personal growth."

Guide to Outdoor Allyship: Part 3

CHOOSE ACTION OVER INACTION

CHOOSE ACTION OVER INACTION. NOT TO DIMINISH YOUR *GOOD* *vibes*, *thoughts and prayers*, or *love and light*, but if you have the opportunity to speak up or act in a way that directly confronts racism, sexism, transphobia, or ableism, do that. Okay, so maybe you're not the ally you thought you were, but you're still reading, which means you care about getting this right. Here are a few steps you can take to fine-tune your allyship.

START WITH YOUR LOCAL COMMUNITY

It's easy to feel overwhelmed by news headlines about global warming, environmental racism targeting Black and Indigenous communities, or, say, hikers littering at your local trailhead. It's natural to feel sad or exhausted by current events. One way to avoid burnout is to get connected with like-minded folks in your local community who care about BIPOC and LGBTQ+ lives as much as they care about eliminating single-use plastics. Affinity groups need your support, and there are several ways you can help that don't require you to take up space.

SUPPORT AFFINITY SPACES

Some outdoor affinity groups are designed to be safe spaces for a particular marginalized community. That's okay. In the same way that veterans need their own groups, sometimes People of Color need communities that are created for and by People of Color. There are definitely individuals who feel threatened by affinity spaces, but you shouldn't be. Whiteness is centered in almost every "positive" or "neutral" aspect of our society. It's okay to cede a few community groups where People of Color can feel seen, heard, and celebrated. Even if a particular space is not intended for you, often there are still ways for you to help by donating money or gently used gear and volunteering time and expertise to build a website, edit a video, or write digital copy. You can also offer mentorship, introduce an editor or industry contact, or share articles online. Another way to get involved is to send a brief email offering a specific skill. This is actually a breath of fresh air for many outdoor affinity groups who receive a constant stream of emails demanding that they work for free.

IF YOU MESS UP, OWN IT

You're going to make mistakes. Own your mistakes, look for lessons learned, and move on. Sometimes moving on takes time. Sometimes it requires you to regain a friend's trust, and sometimes it means regaining an organization's trust or even passing the torch. Sometimes moving on means learning how to take up less space or decentering your own experience as a white person.

TAKE ON A SUPPORTING ROLE

Another good exercise is to be aware of how much space white people take up in a given organization. If you look at authority figures in the United States, they are typically depicted as white, cisgender, and male. The nonprofit space, where 87 percent of executive directors are white, is no exception to the standard of whiteness—even in organizations that do philanthropic work within non-white communities. This is a problem when organizations do not reflect the communities they claim to represent.

Consider the outdoor nonprofit or conservancy where you volunteer: Is the leadership all white or mostly white? Are the board members all white or mostly white? Does the organization partner with subject matter experts and grass-roots leaders who identify as People of Color (POC)? Are the ideas/contributions of POC within the organization valued? Think of the last few POC who left your organization: Was the phrase "just not a good fit" used at the time? When you interact with POC, are they mostly under the age of eighteen? It can be difficult to decenter yourself—especially when society has always reinforced that people who look like you should be in charge—even in areas where you lack grassroots knowledge or the trust of community members. What if you subverted that notion? Instead of leading, what would it look like to take on a supporting role?

SIGNAL BOOST AND PASS THE MIKE

In a recent interview with Melanin Base Camp, nonbinary activist Bam Mendiola spoke about the importance of amplifying and listening to people with intersectional identities who experience multiple forms of oppression. Why? Because we see the world through multiple lenses. We are fluent in whiteness even if you're not fluent in our culture, language, gender identity, or lived experiences. It seems pretty obvious but it's important to recognize that people with marginalized identities have

valuable contributions to make to outdoor recreation and conservation. One way to support POC outdoor leadership is to highlight the work of people who don't look like you, including athletes, activists, filmmakers, small business owners, and creatives. Use your racial privilege and the access you have within outdoor organizations to support those with less privilege and fewer resources.

Lastly, know that sometimes it's appropriate to help tell a marginalized person's story, and sometimes it's not. Sarah Shimazaki, the creator of the *Outside Voices* podcast, talks about ethical storytelling and how telling someone else's story requires time, permission, and relationship building for that to occur.

If at First You Don't Succeed, Take Some Time Off

featuring Dr. Swati Varshney

ELOY, ARIZONA

HOHOKAM, SOBAIPURI-O'ODHAM, AKIMEL O'ODHAM

SHORTLY BEFORE THE WORLD SHUT DOWN IN MARCH 2020, DR. SWATI Varshney boarded a plane with twenty-two other women in the Arizona desert. At 18,000 feet, the pilot leveled off alongside two other aircraft flying in a V formation. Inside the plane, a green light went on and the rear door slid open. Swati felt a blast of cold air as she climbed outside, balancing with several other women on a small ledge while gripping the metal bar on the fuselage with gloved hands.

Shortly afterward, signals flashed between the three planes and women began to fall out of the sky—sixty-six in total, plus a handful of videographers. As she plummeted toward the ground, she was visualizing something that didn't yet exist: an intricate formation of women flying head-down and linked by outstretched arms.

The mission was to build the formation they had rehearsed on the ground that morning and discussed in briefings prior to boarding the three aircraft. Each woman had a specific slot to fill, and they had roughly sixty seconds on the clock before time ran out.

This was the biggest vertical formation skydive of Swati's career thus far. In a way, her 900 jumps and three years of flying head-down had led her to this. At the moment, her task was to free-fall at speeds of up to 180 mph and find her exact slot among the sixty-five other women before "docking." Too fast, and she might sink below the formation or cause waves to ripple through the carefully arranged human domino set. Too slow, and she would miss her chance before the skydivers peeled away.

Swati eased out of a dive as the formation came into view. She waited for her section to build so she could take her assigned position among the other women. As more and more skydivers linked up, Swati moved forward to take grips. Suddenly an audible alarm began to beep in her helmet just as the women around her began to track away. Time was up. Swati turned away, too, swallowing her disappointment. At a safe distance, she pitched her parachute and steered it toward the landing area.

Her love of skydiving began over a decade earlier at a small drop zone in Massachusetts. Soon afterward, she moved to the UK to pursue a master's degree at the University of Cambridge. Over the next year, Swati balanced coursework with traveling around the UK to skydive.

She experienced a lot of firsts—from getting licensed to dropping into pastures filled with sheep or horses when

landings didn't go exactly as planned. Even after she returned to MIT to begin a doctorate in material science and engineering, skydiving remained an important part of her life. "Initially I was drawn to the sport because it was the polar opposite of grad school," said Swati. "I was studying and working in the lab a lot. Skydiving was my escape." Over time, she grew to appreciate the culture that complemented her own love of lifelong learning. Mastering new skills meant traveling around the United States to attend camps and work with instructors in the wind tunnel and in the sky.

In 2019, she first heard about the Project 19 women's world record jump. The plan was for one hundred experienced skydivers to form an intricate aerial formation in celebration of the Nineteenth Amendment's centennial anniversary. Swati had zero experience with big-way skydiving but decided to put herself out there anyway. "I thought, there's no way I'll be ready for that, but I'm willing to take advantage of the training camps and try," she recalled.

Working with mentors and learning new skills was exciting. At the same time, her progression felt like one step forward, two steps back. It didn't come easily, and getting out of her head was a challenge. She learned to deal with disappointment as she struggled with certain skills. "When it came time for the tryout camps, I definitely did not earn an invite," Swati recalled. Then COVID-19 came along and the timeline changed.

Taking time off from the sport during quarantine ironically gave her time to really sit down and think about visualization and the mental aspect—things she hadn't prioritized over the past year of fast-paced camp hopping. She had been struggling with docks throughout all of the Project 19 camps. Now she was back with a stronger-than-ever mental game and a heavier weight belt to help the slender 5'3" skydiver adjust her fall rate.

Swati is still determined to push herself as far as she can go. Receiving a coveted slot on the women's record team would be a major highlight of her skydiving career. In the United States, only 13 percent of skydivers identify as women and a much smaller percentage look like Swati, a brown-skinned first-generation Indian American and the youngest daughter of immigrants. Even if she doesn't make the team, she's already become a much more confident skydiver. "I try to go out of my way to talk to younger women in the sport, to reach out and be a friendly face," she added on her way to coach at an event for women skydivers in North Carolina.

Recently, an energizing talk from professional skydiver Amy Chmelecki helped put her journey into perspective. "I realize that skydiving has its highs and lows," said Swati. "Sometimes things go really well and I progress quickly, and sometimes I make mistakes or I totally screw something up and get cut. Even if I'm feeling low, I know things will get better. It's a good life lesson as well."

Unwelcome Glances

featuring David Robles

SALT LAKE CITY, UTAH

NEWE (SHOSHONE), NEWE (GOSHUTE), NÜÜMÜ, NÚUCHI-U

DAVID ROBLES IS A THIRTY-YEAR-OLD MEXICAN AMERICAN MOUNTAIN biker living in Utah with his partner and two kids. Growing up, he traveled between his home in Utah and Zacatecas, Mexico, where he spent his summers. "The trips to Mexico helped spark my sense of adventure," said David. Life on el rancho was slower paced, and the surrounding countryside was exciting for a city kid on a red Huffy bike.

Back home in West Valley, Salt Lake City, he spent as much time as possible riding, fixing bikes, and watching older kids do dirt jumps in a nearby field. "We would come home from school, eat as fast as we could, go outside, and ride," David recalled.

As he got a little older, he commuted ten miles each day to school and back. Eventually David began showing up to events in the local cycling community. "I started going to critical masses, where people would ride across the entire road and take up space," David recollected. "Back then there was also a 999 road ride; every Thursday at 9:00 p.m. on 9th S and 9th E."

At twenty with zero mountain biking experience, he decided to buy a mountain bike—a Santa Cruz Superlight. David chose a steep trail and had a miserable first time, but he didn't give up. Instead,

he began visiting local bike shops to learn as much as he could about the sport. "I would ask questions and act the part, like I knew what I was doing," said David. His persistence paid off. He learned about different bike groups, the trail color-coding system, and more.

Mountain biking, like many adventure sports, has a lot of hidden knowledge that doesn't come in an owner's manual. It's passed from parent to child, friend to friend, mentor to mentee, or instructor to student. David was starting from scratch without the benefit of any of these options. It's one reason why it can be so challenging to learn an adventure sport when you're the only one who looks like you—oftentimes you're judged for not having knowledge that you don't even have access to as a Person of Color.

David also dealt with unwelcome glances and hostility as one of the few or only brown people on the trail at the time. "People who had started biking at such a young age felt like they had ownership over the mountain biking space, just because they had been exposed to it earlier," David recalled. "It made

me wonder why there weren't as many mountain biking teams on the west side of the valley as there were up in the mountains where there's money."

His identity as a mountain biker has evolved over time from movement-based discovery to community-based advocacy. He still loves the experience of being in nature and exploring his physical strengths and limitations on the trail, but he also enjoys learning about the history of outdoor spaces and the people who have moved through them.

More recently, introducing two small children to the outdoors has been a part of that. "We've gone on camping trips where we end a day early and come home, and we've gone on hikes where we didn't end up at a destination," David admitted. "Overall, it's been really beautiful seeing their smiles and excitement, whether they're on the water, playing in the dirt with their cars and trucks, or hanging out around the fire. Those are really beautiful experiences that I want to continue."

His goal isn't just for his children to have greater access to privileged spaces. David believes that outdoor communities need to become more welcoming spaces where anyone can thrive and gain the knowledge they need to safely recreate.

Lost, Overdue, and Injured Hikers

featuring Kellie R. Torio

SAN GABRIEL MOUNTAINS, CALIFORNIA

YUHAAVIATAM/MAARENGA'YAM (SERRANO), FERNANDEÑO TATAVIAM

SIERRA MADRE SEARCH AND RESCUE TEAM MEMBER KELLIE R. TORIO'S first backpacking trip was in Sequoia National Park. "My pack was only twenty pounds, but at the time it felt like the heaviest thing I had ever carried in my life," she recalled. She brought two extra days' worth of food, a yoga mat, and a 40-degree sleeping bag. At night, the weather promptly dropped below 20 degrees and Kellie lay awake shivering and worrying about wildlife. In the morning when she unzipped her tent flap, she fell in love with the amazing "front porch" view. It's something that stuck with her. She couldn't wait to relive the experience of sleeping under the stars. "I wanted every weekend morning to be like that," Kellie recalled.

She began spending more and more time backpacking and climbing on the weekends. "I had grown up in Los Angeles and was so used to people wanting to party all the time and go to the same clubs every weekend, and that just wasn't me," Kellie explained. Instead, she joined new friends on backpacking trips in the Eastern Sierras and rock-climbing trips to Texas Canyon and Malibu Creek State Park.

Kellie slowly built her confidence with top roping before trying her first multipitch with friends. "Once I got to the top, they were like, 'to get back down you're going to have to rappel.'" Kellie laughed. And that's how she learned to rappel, with the help of friends who ensured that her equipment and technique were correct. That trip led to canyoneering weekends in the San Gabriel Mountains. "It's *almost like* a free water park for people who know how to use rope, harnesses, and belay devices," she added.

Her community became other outdoors people who also worked with their hands and didn't mind getting dirt in their hair. "Meeting people outside felt so seamless," Kellie reminisced. "Everyone I crossed paths with seemed so open and encouraging and supportive. It was my friends who got me outside, but the community is why I stayed."

Her three and a half years on Sierra Madre Search and Rescue have brought together the skills she learned from climbing, backpacking, and canyoneering in the mountains around Los Angeles. "When I first decided to apply, I was like, there's no way I'll make it on the team," Kellie recalled. At the time, she was studying at a fashion institute, and everything on her résumé was fashion-related. Thankfully she was wrong! She ultimately joined the all-volunteer nonprofit whose members have helped locate lost, overdue, and injured hikers since 1951. They also help educate the public regarding hiking safety.

One operation that sticks with her was the rescue of a pair of lost hikers—a man and a woman—who went missing around Cucamonga Peak after one slipped and fell 300 feet. They were reported overdue and remained missing for five days before being located by Kellie's team members in Cucamonga Canyon. After the incident, both hikers learned canyoneering and returned to the site to mark a waypoint of exactly where one had fallen. "One even ended up joining a cave search and rescue team," Kellie added. "In our field, you either really want to help people or you've been rescued and you want to give back. I'm glad it didn't discourage him from the outdoors."

Her advice for lost hikers is to stay put. "It's easier to find someone who isn't moving than to find someone who keeps moving and is a day or two ahead of us," Kellie explained.

The Items They Left Behind

featuring Evan Woodard

BALTIMORE, MARYLAND

SUSQUEHANNOCK, NENTEGO (NANTICOKE) AND PISCATAWAY

ON THE SECOND DAY OF EXCAVATING A 150-YEAR-OLD PRIVY ON A large property in Baltimore, thirty-four-year-old salvage archaeologist Evan Woodard experienced his first cave-in. His team had already finished for the day when, not long after removing the bracing used to support the thirty-foot-deep pit, its walls collapsed in a cloud of dust and crumbling brick. It was an exciting end to a less-than-stellar dig. After two long days of sifting through dirt, trash, and desiccated human manure, one five-gallon Home Depot bucket at a time, his six-man crew had little to show for it. Nearly 900 bucketfuls had been hoisted via tripod pulley system from the bottom of the dig to the surface, where team members carefully examined its contents to find a few stoneware items, a whiskey flask, and a medication bottle.

At a second excavation site on the property, Evan would later salvage one of his favorite finds in his eighteen-month career as a privy digger: a boot pistol of late-nineteenth-century vintage with a single intact shot. It was the kind owned by women and gamblers and prized for its size and easy concealment. "Women would put these in their purses or stockings, and gamblers kept them up their sleeves," said Evan. "It's a single shot but it packed a hell of a punch."

Evan did not set out to be a privy digger. Originally from Laurel, Maryland, he grew up with a love of all things history before making a career in cybersecurity. "I still did a lot of urban exploring through abandoned buildings, tunnels, and sewers, looking for history, writing stories, and documenting what I found," said Evan. It wasn't until the pandemic hit that he discovered his vocation as a salvage archaeologist. He was looking for something to do when he saw a friend's social media post about hiking and finding old bottles. "Pretty soon, I wasn't just finding items; I was telling the stories of who owned them and uncovering real histories," Evan summarized.

After a few false starts exploring dumps around the city of Baltimore, Evan and a friend found their calling as privy diggers. They learned that outhouses used to double as trash cans. "A privy in your yard was a private space," said Evan.

It was easy enough to select an area by learning the history of Baltimore's neighborhoods and tapping into Maryland's online database. The next step—convincing homeowners to let them dig on their property—was less difficult than one would think, said the salvage archaeologist. "People are really open once they understand that it's a historical thing."

Evan typically carries items from past excavations—a perfectly preserved flask or beer bottle—with him on his door-to-door pitches. After obtaining permission, he uses a Sanborn Fire Insurance Map from 1870 to the 1880s to determine the original property line. If he's lucky, the location of the outhouse might appear on the map. Afterward, Evan uses a long piece of spring steel attached to a metal T-post to probe the soil and gauge the level of resistance. Even though the wooden superstructure has long since rotted away and even though the privy shaft has been capped with clay, ash, or debris, there are still obvious signs. "The soil is going to be really soft compared to the earth around it," said Evan. "If the probe goes in super smooth, you're inside a privy. You find the walls first and then start digging."

The 6'5" amateur historian doesn't typically fit inside of the pits, which tend to be four to five feet in diameter and up to thirty feet deep. "I'm usually the one pulling buckets up," Evan explained. "A lot of times, you'll see us and mounds of dirt behind us and it's really just dried human feces. Thankfully it doesn't smell when it's dry." And at the end of the painstaking process, he's also the one cleaning and documenting items and, in certain cases, donating them to local institutions like the Baltimore Museum of Industry. Pistols are a rare find. Flasks are much more common. "They're cylindrical, so they have more strength to them than other discarded items," said Evan. "When you do find them, you're amazed that something this fragile has lasted well over 125 or 150 years, looking as if they just came from the factory." At home, his collection of mint-condition bottles, flasks, decanters, along with the weirder finds—animal bones and boar tusks—is a testament to the range of items that ended up discarded in nineteenth-century toilets.

The stories Evan tells in his account are mostly those of white families, "but there's the occasional story of a Black man, woman, or child," Evan added. That sort of erasure is due to structural racism, including the eminent domain seizure and destruction of historic Black neighborhoods to make way for industrial development projects, highways, and gentrification. While it's true that nineteenth-century Baltimore's bustling shipyards drew freed Blacks from across the region, much of their presence has been erased over the past 150 years.

The irony isn't lost on him. "If you look at the historical record, there's a huge drop-off in information once you get closer to 1880—if you're Black," said Evan. "It doesn't make sense that we can't find out our own history. You can learn the history of white migrant communities in Baltimore, but it's a lot harder if you're Black or Native American."

There are other options outside of Baltimore. Evan has an excavation site on a former plantation in northern Maryland. However, even that has proved frustrating. "There was terrible record keeping when it came to the enslaved people who lived there," he said. "I found the original privy for the big house, but I'm still trying to locate the slave quarters."

He's not giving up, and even though he realizes that digging through 150-year-old outhouses won't appeal to everyone, Evan wants to encourage Black, Indigenous, and other People of Color to give it a try. "It's a predominantly white man's hobby, and they're all older," said Evan. "We really *are* the next generation; that's why it's important to get more people into it." The reward is learning about the lives of the people who lived here before us through the items they left behind.

Brown Girls
Climb

featuring Bethany Lebewitz

STEELE, ALABAMA

SHAWANWAKI/SHAWNEE, S'ATSOYAHA (YUCHI)

IN 2020 IN NORTHERN ALABAMA, THREE HUNDRED CLIMBERS OF color gathered for a weekend of bouldering, food, and music—the first of its kind. One of the event organizers was Bethany Lebewitz, a thirty-three-year-old Mexican American from Cut and Shoot, Texas. She is known across the climbing industry as a change-maker, activist, and businessperson whose company, Brown Girls Climb, is redefining the climbing experience.

Bethany grew up as a biracial Latina in a third-generation Mexican American family in rural Texas. She spent her summers fishing, digging for crawdads, and swimming at state parks. Despite her strong connection to nature, her childhood was challenging in other ways. "We had our struggles," she added. "I worried about getting caught up in the cycle."

After high school, she moved to Latin America, where she taught art. She began rock climbing while living in Ecuador. "Climbing was very helpful in reminding me that even if I don't make it to the top, I've made these little progressions along the way," she reflected. "Before, I hadn't had anything tangible to reflect that in my life. It was also helpful for me as a first-generation college applicant as I applied to school and was dealing with anxiety."

After graduating with a degree in neuroscience and childhood early

development, Bethany ended up in the Washington, DC, area in 2016, in search of friends and new climbing partners. That was when she decided to start an Instagram account called Brown Girls Climb. "I'm kind of an introvert," she added. "I thought this would give me an excuse to talk to other women of Color. I could take pictures and start a conversation about what was happening politically, but we could also climb."

From there, things moved quickly. She cohosted the first Color the Crag meetup in October 2017 with Mikhail Martin from Brothers of Climbing. "It was so radically different from the climbing space that existed and from what was culturally available," she recalled. "There was a single template out there that gyms and festivals used that centered whiteness and white men—lots of bro-y misogyny." Instead of following that template, they chose to create something new. Eighty climbers attended the first Color the Crag event in Alabama, including several Black and brown athletes who were paid to lead clinics.

From there, things moved quickly. She helped create a team of regional leaders—women climbers from around the country "who saw how deeply entrenched white supremacy was in this space" and who believed in the conversations she helped facilitate on race, gender, and queer POC representation, on and off the rock. "There's power in numbers," Bethany pointed out, and each new wave of Color the Crag attendees was returning to their local communities to continue the movement. New organizations for climbers of Color began emerging across the country.

Brown Girls Climb rolled out a national membership model in 2019, followed by the Brown Girls Climb app in 2020. Then in 2021, in the midst of the pandemic, she successfully crowdfunded over $108,000 to launch the BGC Marketplace—a values-based online shopping experience that aims to help consumers connect with companies and products that represent their social values. That means promoting corporate responsibility, adaptive products, and inclusive sizing alongside LGBTQ+-owned and BIPOC-owned companies.

Bethany believes BGC Marketplace will ultimately invest back into marginalized communities. It's a new way of doing business in an industry that has a bad habit of treating People of Color as props instead of as people. "There is the beauty of building something yourself from scratch," said Bethany. "You can think about building something whose infrastructure has accountability."

A Sense of Belonging

featuring John Shin

DENVER, COLORADO

HINONO'EINO (ARAPAHO), TSISTSISTAS (CHEYENNE), NÚUCHI-U (UTE), OČHÉTHI ŠAKÓWIŊ)

JOHN SHIN IS A KOREAN AMERICAN CLIMBER LIVING IN DENVER, Colorado, where he recently put down roots after years on the road. He didn't grow up spending a lot of time outdoors. Instead, his childhood in Tuckahoe, New York, was centered around his family's dry-cleaning business. "My parents worked twelve hours a day, six days a week," said John. He helped out by sweeping floors, steaming pants, tagging clothes, and working the register. "Looking back, I think it was important to have seen what my parents had to do every day," said John. "It's made me more connected with their immigrant experience."

That doesn't mean his relationship with his parents was easy. He even joined the U.S. Army Reserve in college as a means of getting out from under his father, who viewed the parent-child relationship as more transactional than John would've liked. "He dictated things to me; there were no conversations," said John. "Everything hinged upon my academic performance. He threatened that if I didn't get a certain GPA, I would not be continuing school there."

His other reason for joining the army was harder to admit at the time. "There was an element of being emasculated as an Asian American man and wanting

to redeem myself through the military—wanting to prove my Americanness," John confessed. At thirty-one, he feels much more confident in his identity. However, it still occasionally causes him to pick apart his motive for seemingly neutral decisions like buying a pickup truck or throwing himself into vanlife and climbing across North America. It sometimes is difficult to escape the impulse to prove himself, especially when racial bigotry means his identity and masculinity are constantly up for debate.

After college, John began climbing at a local gym. He had never been very athletic, but the lanky six-footer found himself progressing quickly. John worked on gaining new technical skills through classes, like lead climbing, and transferring those skills to climbing outdoors on sandstone and granite.

After a few months, he crossed over into traditional, or "trad" climbing, a style of climbing that involves placing and removing protection as you go instead of relying upon bolts drilled into the rock. It's a higher-risk side of the sport, and John relished it.

John found trad teachers here and there before deciding to quit his job and pursue climbing full time as a vanlifer. For seven months, he drove across North America visiting popular sites for experienced trad climbers in the Southwest United States, as well as in Canada and Mexico. In doing so, he was following a blueprint long established in the sport: elective poverty or "dirt bagging" as the *lifestyle* option for those who wanted more than weekends at the crag and weeknights at the local climbing gym.

Climbing full time and choosing to live out of your vehicle is romanticized by many climbers. In reality, it's not a glamorous lifestyle. John enjoyed having the opportunity to climb every day, the freedom of the open road, along with the new people and experiences that came with it. However, he was still haunted by a sense of not belonging. He also spent long stretches alone with his thoughts, trying to process memories, including the internalized racism that he had dealt with his entire life.

There was a moment of personal crisis in Squamish, British Columbia. He had just finished reading *Between the World and Me* by Ta-Nehisi Coates. "Obviously, it's about the Black experience, but it made me realize a lot of things about myself," John recalled. As he read, the sense of alienation that he had lived with for much of his life felt overwhelming. He tried discussing it with his parents but got nowhere. Instead, John wrote an article about his experience of being an Asian American man in the overwhelmingly white climbing community. The article went viral. That was in 2016.

It was a weird time for John. He definitely lost a few friendships over it but strengthened others. "I think if those friends hadn't grown along with me, perhaps we wouldn't be talking now," said John. He also placed renewed effort into his relationship with his parents. "I'm not sure my parents have ever really cared to understand how much of a thing climbing is in my life," John confessed. "Yes, they think it's dangerous and don't want to know, but they also generally don't care about my passions—only my financial well-being and security." In the years that followed, he gradually accepted that the way his parents expressed love was shaped by the financial insecurity they experienced

as immigrants, just as his own impulse to prove himself was shaped by the racism and alienation he experienced.

In that way, climbing has brought him closer to where he started. His years on the road, in the army, in the Peace Corps, and as a vanlifer and dirtbag climber were fueled by a desire for belonging and validation. "Before, I was always thinking about my next move," said John. "Where am I going to go? What am I going to do? What can I check off my list?" Accepting this about himself was a weight off his shoulders. It also empowered him to make his identity as a Korean American climber his own.

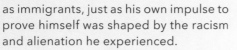

"What has also changed about me in the past few years is how good I feel around other people and how committed I am to creating safe spaces for people I care about," said John. Recently, that has meant climbing with People of Color and offering his skills as a "trad" mentor. Instead of specific climbing routes or projects, he's focusing outward on building community. Teaching makes him a stronger climber. It's also his small way of shifting the climbing scene toward a more accepting environment.

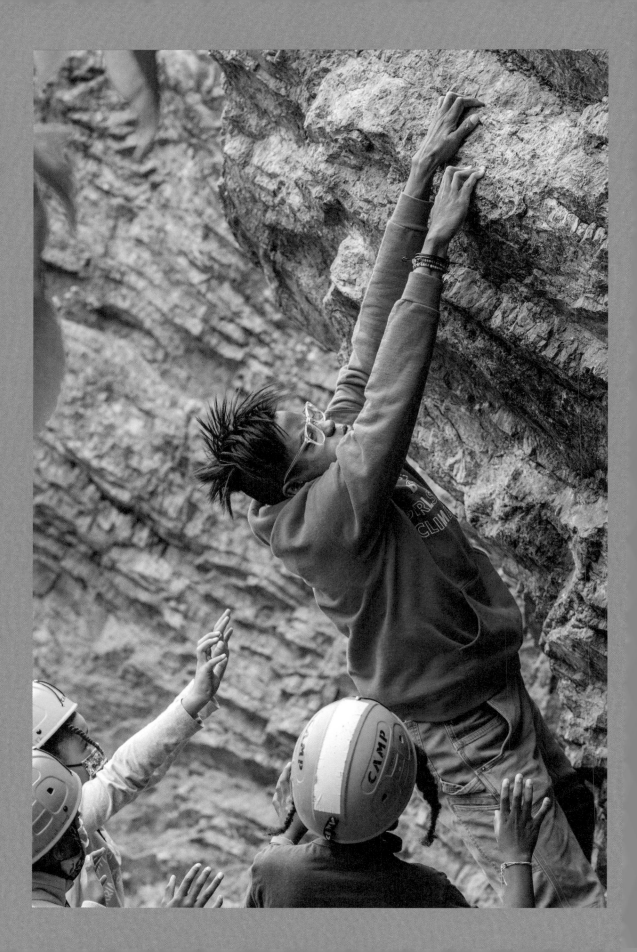

How to Take Up Space as a Black Queer Woman

featuring Emily Taylor

OAKLAND, CALIFORNIA

**CONFEDERATED VILLAGES OF LISJAN-OHLONE
AND MUWEKMA-OHLONE**

EMILY TAYLOR IS A FORTY-SEVEN-YEAR-OLD BLACK QUEER PROFES-sional climbing coach based in Oakland, California. She's also the CEO of Taylored Fit Solutions and founder of a youth climbing program for Black, Indigenous Girls of Color.

Her nearly three decades of experience in the industry have covered a lot of firsts. In 2003, Emily became the first Black woman to successfully climb the Nose, a climbing route on El Capitan in Yosemite National Park. During that time, she was also the first Black female regional leader for USA Climbing, a position she held

for twelve years while leading adaptive climbing efforts for the Southeast United States and coaching former youth prodigy turned professional climber Kai Lightner for seven years.

The youngest daughter of a Marine Corps colonel, Emily was raised in a strict single-parent military household at bases in Okinawa; Kuwait; Iwakuni, Japan; and Quantico, Virginia. She enrolled at Winthrop University in Rock Hill, South Carolina. Being Black and openly gay in the early '90s wasn't easy. Then her dad died during her junior year of college. "I buried him on my twenty-first birthday," said Emily. "And that's how I entered adulthood—in survival mode." As a way to deal with her grief, she signed up for her first Outward Bound course, a two-month Colorado adventure that involved kayaking, canoeing, and rock climbing. She later described it as "the first time, athletically, that things came together in my body." Emily discovered that she had a natural affinity for climbing, and the positive affirmations she received from instructors chipped away at the feelings of never being good enough that had haunted her during her childhood.

Emily began climbing regularly at a Black-owned gym in nearby Charlotte, North Carolina. She also joined a climbing gym in Pensacola, Florida, where she made frequent trips to care for her

grandmother. After college, she moved to Atlanta, which felt like a relative safe haven for a queer Black woman climber. By then she was competing, coaching, and designing youth climbing programs. Working in the industry combined her love of teaching and working with children. "To find something that involved movement and that I was physically really good at was also healing," said Emily.

At the same time, the mostly white male climbing community could be very lonely. "My climbing region was Kentucky, Virginia, West Virginia, Alabama, and Tennessee," she explained. "Being with all straight white dudes in that outdoor environment was isolating." It was also discomforting to have to rely upon white people for her safety in that environment. Even though growing up as a military kid gave her a certain level of code-switching and knowledge about moving within white communities, that didn't erase the more unsettling aspects of climbing culture—such as the first time someone introduced their wife as their "belay slave" or the many climbing routes with racially insensitive names.

"Spending time in white male spaces where your identity isn't centered is challenging," said Emily. Over the years, she's dealt with verbal abuse from parents, racial slurs, and organizations that want the window dressing of Black people without having to listen to Black voices. She's also formed deep connections while working with youth climbers. "Working with clients is like a grounding force," she summarized. These days, she mostly coaches brown girls and autistic youth, and after years of dealing with gym politics, she's excited to have a space to call home—a free-to-use private training facility where she can provide private coaching without worrying about the microaggressions that her clients would otherwise face in predominantly white spaces.

When Your Outdoor Friends Are Not Good Allies

Let's talk about a sensitive topic we tend to shy away from.

If you're a Person of Color active in backcountry outdoor sports, it's possible that your partner is white and most of your outdoorsy friends are too. No, this doesn't apply to everyone—but it does apply to a lot of us. It's a simple fact of the mountain towns we live in and how we choose to spend our time. The outdoor communities many of us turn to after work and on the weekends and during trips throughout the year are not integrated. They are very, very white, and oftentimes, we find ourselves as the "only Black girl" or the "only Asian guy" or the "only queer Woman of Color" in the group. You may gradually find yourself spending more and more time in predominantly white spaces and less and less time around people who look like you. Many of us have diverse circles of friends only on social media and a few times each year, when we catch up with friends from high school or college. It's one reason why online affinity groups are so important. So how do you know if your outdoor friends are good allies? And what do you do if they're not? I have very few answers for the second question, but I can help you with the first. Here are six reasons why your outdoor friends may be taxing the hell out of your emotional health.

1. They come and tell you about racist comments they overheard and chose not to respond to.

Or they'll send you screenshots of racist comments on Instagram. They want recognition for correctly identifying the thing as racist, but it either doesn't occur to them or they simply choose not to step up in the moment. They aren't anti-racist around their coworkers or friends or fellow outdoors enthusiasts. They're silent. They've correctly identified you as the person who will say or do something about it, but they're not willing to do that work themselves.

2. Your novice mistakes are constantly misattributed to your race or gender.

You biffed one landing at the drop zone, and now they won't shut up about how girls can't fly parachutes—even though your wing-loading is higher than theirs and you've been flying high-performance canopies since you became a licensed skydiver. You are called into the front office and have to sit through a lecture about safety. Plot twist: your best friend in the sport is white and male. After he breaks his tib-fib on a reckless low turn, an experienced instructor at the drop zone takes him under his wing and teaches him advanced canopy piloting, free of charge. His friends laugh it off, and six months later, no one is talking about it. That's called failing up. It's a special power that many white cisgender men have. Your mom is originally from the Philippines and six months later, you're still listening to nonstop jokes about how "Asian girls" can't fly parachutes. The thought of making another mistake, any mistake, is making you sick to your stomach. Maybe you won't learn high-performance landings after all. Maybe you'll just play it safe for the rest of your life.

3. "Not trying to be offensive, but . . . " always precedes an offensive remark.

You don't want to speak up because the speakers are funny and well-liked by the other bros. Or they took you on your first traditional climb, and damn if the community isn't hard to break into. This is your chance! How many more memes about social justice warriors and jokes about safe spaces are you going to have to put up with? Maybe you're white passing or not visibly queer, and because of that everyone assumes you must be white and straight. So you hear and see everything. Every homophobic joke. Every racist meme.

At night around the campfire, your friend frequently refers to his ex-wife using offensive slurs in front of you. You want to ask him to stop, but you also want to say nothing and just be "one of the guys." You don't want to speak up and ruin the vibe, especially when you're new to the group and no one else is taking offense. So, you just stay quiet instead. He's never said anything personally offensive about you, so it's okay, right? You'll just keep your head down for another few months and you'll be fine.

4. They gaslight you all the time.

If something racist happens to you at the trailhead, in the parking lot, or in the climbing gym, you have no one to talk to—that is, no one who will believe you. Your friends don't understand because they are unable and unwilling to empathize with anything that doesn't personally affect them. They tell you that you're misreading the situation or exaggerating. When you get pulled over by cops on the first leg of your epic outdoor adventure, they tell you to brush it off—it could've happened to anyone. When you get pulled over by cops on the second leg of your epic outdoor adventure, they blame your out-of-state plates. You let one of your friends drive for the rest of the trip and try to forget about it.

When you feel unsafe holding hands with your same-sex partner on the trail, your friends tell you to loosen up. But you don't feel safe. You're tired of being stared at. You are scared of being visibly queer at rest stops, gas stations, and trailheads. They say you're being too emotional, or they explain that you're the problematic one for talking about homophobia so much. Nature doesn't care what you look like or who you're with. Right?

5. They tone-police your emotional response to racism, homophobia, and transphobia.

You've never had so many white people you barely know quote Martin Luther King Jr. at you—usually whitewashed quotes taken out of context. Real allies prioritize anti-racism over tone-policing how they think People of Color should respond to racism, but by now, you're starting to suspect that your friends aren't real allies. They don't understand why you're crying and don't feel like climbing after reading about the latest police shooting of an unarmed Black man or the unsolved murder of another Indigenous woman.

They aggressively tone-police you on social media, demanding that you respond to racists in a nicer tone if you expect to be heard.

They whine about how safe spaces and affinity groups violate their First Amendment rights. They refuse to check other people in the group who intentionally misgender you or who make openly racist comments. They are constantly prioritizing their comfort over your emotional well-being and safety.

6. Your friends confuse being nice with being anti-racist.

You know they're not the same, but now you're not so sure if your friends understand the difference. They actively avoid talking about race. They say things like "Why do we have to be Black and white? Why can't we just be people?" Or they insist that they don't see color and explain how it's more important to just be a good person. That matters more than all this racial stuff. If you mention a creepy interaction you had with someone else in the group, your friend reminds you that so-and-so is a good person with a wife and kid. You're not exactly sure what that is supposed to mean.

Your friends encourage you to "be happy, and stop talking about race all the time" when you try to tell them about a white gas station owner who falsely accuses you of stealing. They think you're

a drag on the conversation when you mention the stares you and your white girlfriend received on the trail. They pass you another beer and someone quickly changes the topic.

7. You are emotionally exhausted from microaggressions and code-switching all the time.

Your outdoor friends think acrylics are ghetto, so you don't get them anymore. They think your music is ghetto, so you stop listening to it around them. They think your Walmart tent is too heavy and your sleeping bag is too bulky, so you upgrade to ultralight gear and charge everything on your credit card. Now you look like you're ready to climb K2, even though you only car camp occasionally with friends. You prefer styling your hair naturally, but your friends think it looks better straight. You like protective styles, but the one time you wore box braids on a camping trip, they asked, "How does your hair grow so fast?" and kept trying to touch it. They think it's funny that you're patting your head and they demand to know why you have to wrap your hair up at night or why you won't go swimming with them. New people in the group frequently signal how progressive they are by asking you "Where are you really from?" Or they greet you in Spanish to show that they are cultured and self-aware enough to recognize your Latinx surname. But you don't speak Spanish and didn't grow up speaking it. Your parents wanted to protect you from the racism they experienced daily at grocery stores, banks, and doctors' offices for speaking Spanish or having accented English. You notice that none of your white friends ever get asked where they're really from. And no one randomly greets them in German or French. But your friends are just being nice, right? And that's the most important thing… being a nice person. Your friends mispronounce your birth name so you shorten it to something easier for them to say. They like showing off that they have a Muslim friend, as if you're a centerpiece or conversation starter. They ask a lot of questions about Ramadan and even fast for a few days in solidarity, but when you want to talk about Muslims being killed in Gaza or imprisoned in China, their eyes glaze over with disinterest.

OKAY, SO SOME OF YOUR PROGRESSIVE FRIENDS ARE PROBLEMATIC

What are you supposed to do? It's not your job to fix them, right? They don't see race because it's never been a barrier for them. They don't like talking about race because as children they were taught that the mere acknowledgment of race, or disability, or any kind of difference is bad. They aren't arrogant; they just think that if something isn't affecting them personally, it can't be affecting anyone else, right? They center themselves in every conversation because society centers them—that's why they have trouble making space for others.

They were raised to think that their opinion matters most and that racism doesn't really exist if they say it doesn't. They are defensive and angry and also afraid of messing up. And they're your friends. And they took you on your first fourteener and your first snowboarding trip to Mammoth, and you even hiked the High Sierra Trail together. They're your good friends from college. They introduced you to your partner. They were in your wedding. No one's perfect, right? Right?

Winter Training Selfies

featuring Stephanie Vu

DENVER, COLORADO

HINONO'EINO (ARAPAHO), TSISTSISTAS (CHEYENNE), NÚUCHI-U (UTE), OČHÉTHI ŠAKÓWIƞ

STEPHANIE VU IS A MULTISPORT ATHLETE WHO ENJOYS ELK HUNTING, biathlon, cross-country skiing, downhill skiing, trail running, and skimo. Prior to that, the thirty-three-year-old intellectual property lawyer grew up in Chalmette, a small town outside of New Orleans, Louisiana. Her childhood was spent fishing and jet-skiing on Lake Pontchartrain or riding dirt bikes.

She and her siblings also grew up skiing in Aspen and Durango. They were one of the few students in their grammar school to see snow or travel that far west. Between the twenty-one-hour drives to Colorado ski country and the annual visits to national parks like the Grand Canyon, Glacier, and Yellowstone, she felt ready to leave the Gulf Coast behind. Then Hurricane Katrina hit, flooding her childhood home and displacing her parents to Dallas, Texas. Instead of relocating out west, Stephanie decided to remain close by for college. Afterward, she went

to Patagonia, the southernmost region in South America, for a month of solo backpacking.

The trip was inspired by a travel blog featuring the famed W Trek through the granite towers, alpine lakes, and southern ice fields of Torres del Paine National Park. She stayed in hostels in Chile and Argentina and hiked alone for the first time in her life. "One time, a father and son asked where I was going and when I told them, they shook their heads and told me I was going the wrong way," Stephanie recollected. "I followed them through these really tall bushes only to emerge on the opposite end covered in caterpillars." Her guides pointed her in the right direction and she resumed her hike. This was a pre-smartphone era, and serendipitous moments like these were a reminder that she was exactly where she needed to be—trying new experiences on her own with the confidence and curiosity that she had inherited from her parents.

Not long after returning to the United States, she began applying to law schools out west. "I felt that my parents were in a better place, and this was my chance to fulfill a childhood dream by moving to Colorado," she explained. Stephanie and her partner packed up their lives in Texas and drove to Denver. The next step was to put down roots in a state known for its outdoor culture. She started with activities she had always wanted to try, like cross-country skiing. "When I was a kid, my parents would say, 'We didn't drive twenty-one hours for you to cross-country ski,'"—she laughed—"'We drove twenty-one hours for you to downhill ski.'"

She and her partner were in the middle of lessons at a local ski resort when she spotted someone with a biathlon rifle skiing to the range. "I was like, 'Oh, that looks cool; I'm going to check it out,'" said Stephanie. One thing led to another, and she soon found herself in a biathlon safety class. It wasn't until halfway through that she leaned over to her partner and asked, "Why are they talking about this like these are real rifles?" His response shocked her: "That's because they are." That was the moment she realized that biathletes competed with actual .22-caliber rifles.

Stephanie soon discovered that she loved shooting—and, of course, hitting her targets on her very first day definitely didn't hurt. The emphasis on two very different skill sets, skiing and shooting, also enthralled her. "With skiing, you're going as hard as you can and elevating your heart rate; with shooting, it's like, okay I need to calm down and time everything just right," Stephanie explained. "I appreciate the balance between the two."

Over time, biathlon became a gateway to other sports like skimo, a form of uphill skiing. "They're basically ultralight skis geared toward moving fast uphill that can be reconfigured for downhill skiing," said Stephanie. "There's a ski for every condition!" Her social media is full of biathlon and skimo winter training selfies with frozen eyelashes, puffy jackets, and dark, snowy vistas. Stephanie is currently training for the Grand Traverse, a forty-mile backcountry ski race with a vertical gain of 6,800 feet. After a teammate's injury derailed a 2021 attempt, she is excited about getting back out there.

Biathlon helped Stephanie find a community in Colorado that also included hunting. After firing her first .22 rifle, she tried a shotgun and then a hunting rifle before settling on a recurve bow. However, her personal interest in hunting began years before she started competing in biathlon. "After reading *The*

Omnivore's Dilemma, I wanted to be more conscientious about the meat that I consumed and where it comes from," she explained. "At the time, I was like, I can't hunt, so I'll just become a vegetarian." She eventually began purchasing meat locally from farmers' markets, but her interest in hunting remained. Biathlon helped reopen the conversation. "I thought, well, now that I can shoot a rifle, maybe I can hunt," Stephanie added.

After her partner began bow hunting, Stephanie picked up the sport and they started to hunt elk together as a couple. That was a few years ago. Each new season means shooting her bow once a week to work her way back up to its draw weight. It also means getting to know the public land available to them. They hunt public-over-the-counter, which means that after a limited draw, or lottery, licenses have to be purchased for big game like elk. Even though the archery season lasts for only thirty days each September, a lot of preparation goes into it.

Stephanie and her partner spend a lot of time hiking off-trail and familiarizing themselves with different hunting areas prior to the start of the season. "Early on, we typically scout an area, walk around, and see if it makes sense that elk might be here in two months," said Stephanie. "There's no substitute for walking the land."

Hunting also surprised her by how much it forced her to slow down and really look around. "Whether I'm looking for signs on trees, tracks on the ground, scat, or fur, I really started to look at my surroundings," she recalled. "Now when I'm out in the woods, even when I'm not hunting, I feel like I'm taking in a lot more." It's not that she doesn't do destination-focused hiking or trail running—she does—but she also appreciates the ability to slow down and view nature through a different lens.

Scouting on the map versus scouting in person can sometimes be very different. It requires them to consider factors like cattle fences, impassable ravines, weather, possible spoilage, distance, and speed—all important variables that go into decision making. "Hunting is so much more than shooting an animal and taking it home," said Stephanie. "I haven't gotten one yet, but I have had an encounter when a bull came within ten feet of me. It was one of the most incredible experiences of my life." Many elk hunters venture out each season and never even set eyes on their prey. For Stephanie, it's still worth the effort. She's grown to appreciate the off-trail hiking, frigid early mornings, and long, sweltering days.

She and her partner typically hike in at 3:00 a.m., set up in the trees, and sit for as long as possible, hoping the intelligent, easily spooked animals don't catch wind of them. "I just love them because they're so smart," Stephanie gushed. "A deer has a one-mile radius that they'll run around in when they get spooked. Once you startle an elk, they're gone. They're like, 'Well, we'll just go to the next valley.'"

It's rare that Stephanie comes across other Asian American women in biathlon, backcountry skiing, or hunting, much less another second-generation Vietnamese American daughter of immigrants. Her parents aren't exactly thrilled either when it comes to her choices in outdoor recreation. "I actually don't tell my parents a lot about what I do," Stephanie confessed. "The few times I tried, my mom was like, 'This makes me worry, it sounds dangerous, I don't want to hear about it.'" Her parents immigrated to the United States

during the Vietnam War and simply have a different perspective of leisure activities that doesn't include enduring freezing temperatures while dressed in head-to-toe camouflage. At the same time, they raised her to be confident and independent and to not care about what other people think.

"My dad did a really good job of instilling in me the confidence to be able to trust myself," said Stephanie. "Yes, he's like, 'Why would you put yourself through that voluntarily?' but sometimes his response is 'Oh that's cool!'"

Her advice to newcomers is to find groups that offer support and community like women-only hunts or dirt biking rides—she's done both! "Most people in those groups are very welcoming to beginners," said Stephanie. "They understand what it's like to be new and how intimidating that can feel."

Surviving
a Plane Crash

featuring Will Middlebrooks

STATESBORO, GEORGIA

MVSKOKE (MUSCOGEE / CREEK)

THE MORNING OF THE PLANE CRASH, WILL MIDDLEBROOKS COM-pleted two uneventful skydives with friends over a small airport in Central Georgia. It wasn't their usual drop zone since that location's runways were closed for maintenance, but it was similar. In addition, a brand-new jump pilot was filling in behind the controls of the Cessna 182. "Otherwise it was a normal day," said Will. The skies were clear and temperatures were climbing toward the high 80s. Life was good.

In fact, the only other thing out of place was the missing fuel cap on the right wing fuel tank. After conferring, the pilot and an airport mechanic decided on a makeshift cover. The plane made one more successful flight before Will boarded the aircraft for the third time since his arrival that morning. Soon after, he was joined by three additional skydivers—a U.S. Army demonstration parachutist, a tandem instructor and father of three, and a skydiving student and father of two. The twenty-three-year-old pilot sat up front.

"I had 211 jumps that day," said Will. "We got into the aircraft like we normally do, and I shut my eyes and relaxed." Shortly after takeoff, the familiar sound of the engine suddenly went quiet. His next memory was of waking up in the intensive care unit at Augusta University Hospital.

Will was born in 1995 at Tripler Army Medical Center in Hawai'i to two military parents. His family eventually relocated to Augusta, Georgia, where he spent most of his childhood. That was followed by a mechanical engineering degree from Georgia Southern University, close to the Statesboro Airport, where he completed his first tandem skydive at age twenty-one. Becoming a licensed jumper was just the start. He eventually obtained his instructor ratings. "I became a tandem instructor in order to bring new people into the sport and give them the experience I had on my very first skydive," said Will. To date, he's taken over 300 students on their very first jump.

Skydiving also exposed him to aerial videography and photography. He wears a Sony a6000 mounted on his helmet and utilizes a hands-free shutter release called a *blow switch* to take midair photos of customers. It requires him to blow into a thumb-sized plastic tube while free-falling at 120 mph. He usually has forty-five seconds to capture the photos he needs for each jump—plus a second camera to capture footage of the skydive, as well as the skydivers' prejump jitters and postjump euphoria.

Shooting video and stills for tandem skydives has become his favorite part of the sport. "Before each jump, there's a moment when the person realizes that it's the first time they've been in a plane with the door open—and their facial expression is priceless," said Will. His job is to hang outside of the aircraft at 12,000 feet and capture those first impressions, ranging from calm to excitement to terror. "Everyone wants to look straight down as they get closer to the door," Will explained. It's a dividing line between safety and uncertainty. It can take a lot of

courage to cross it—but it's worth it, Will argues.

There's a crucial moment, just after the tandem student leaves the aircraft, when their fear is replaced by smiles and laughter. He captures that too. "The fear stays in the plane," said Will. "The moment they leave the plane, it's nothing but joy."

Will has no memory of the fear he felt during the plane crash or the relief of being rescued from the burning wreckage. "I only know what they told me," he explained.

According to official reports, the small plane lost engine power for unknown reasons during takeoff, pitched downward, and dove 150 feet into the ground. It came to rest beyond the end of the runway, where it burst into flames. Will, who had been seated in the back of the aircraft at the time of the crash, was the only

survivor. He was pulled from the twisted metal of the fuselage by Dean Gowen, a local man who had been golfing only moments before witnessing the crash. Dean immediately jumped a fence and was the first to arrive at the scene.

Will woke up later that evening at a nearby trauma hospital ICU with a broken neck, internal bleeding, a collapsed lung, burns, lacerations, and a shattered ankle. "Waking up was that stereotypical movie scene where everything is blurry and it's slowly coming into focus," he recalled. "As soon as your eyes open, there are people coming up to you and asking a bunch of questions. I realized that I had been in a plane and that now I was in a hospital. I put the rest together." He was unable to move, his leg was too swollen for surgery, and a chest tube was draining the blood from around his collapsed lung into a device below his bed. "Every time a nurse or doctor would come in, they would look under the bed at the drainage before they would address me," said Will. "Everyone had the same grim look on their face."

A few days later, he received the news that he was the only survivor. "The drop zone owner called me," Will recalled. "My parents and the medical staff were trying to get the phone away from me and she ended up telling me before they could." Afterward, he dealt with a lot of survivor's guilt. "I was thinking, 'Why me? Why not anyone else?'" said Will. "I had a lot of deep sadness at that point."

Around ten days into his hospital stay, Will began experiencing an unfamiliar pressure in his chest whenever he sat up that doctors dismissed as anxiety. Days later, when he took his first step on crutches outside of his hospital room, his heart rate spiked and monitor alarms began going off. "Everyone showed up because they thought I was about to have a heart attack," said Will. "That's when the doctors started taking it seriously; that's when the conversation about swelling around my heart started." He wound up back in the intensive care unit for another surgery to drain the fluid that had built up around his heart.

Despite the setback, Will was eventually released from the hospital after a five-week stay. While he recovered at home over the next few months, the pull of the drop zone was always in the back of his mind. "Once I was back home, people were asking me if I was going to jump again," said Will. "I had the idea of returning to skydiving but I didn't have it all figured out yet. On the other hand, I didn't want to become afraid of flying either."

After his cast came off, he began showing up at the drop zone on weekends to say hi and help out. His friends pushed him to do a jump. "I was making every excuse in the book: 'Nah, I don't have my rig, it's with the manufacturer' and 'I don't have my helmet,'" Will recalled. "Of course their responses were 'Here, use my rig' and 'You can use my helmet.'" He ended up making a jump that day.

As he preflighted his gear, he began to have a panic attack. "My heart was racing; I felt like everything was moving all at once—really fast," Will recalled. After he boarded the plane, everything slowed back down again. He closed his eyes and relaxed. "Once the plane door opened at 12,000 feet, it was business as usual," said Will. "I ended up landing on one leg."

Replacing his gear that had been destroyed both by the accident and the EMTs' life-saving measures turned out to be simpler than expected. Skydiving gear manufacturers sent him custom replacements or repaired his damaged gear free of charge. The hard part was reintegrating into the community. "Prior to the accident, I was "that Black skydiver," said Will, who skydives in rural Georgia. "Afterward I became 'that Black skydiver who survived a plane crash'—hyper visible." Strangers would approach him at events just to talk about the accident. "I didn't mind so long as they were respectful," Will explained. "Talking about it is actually kind of therapeutic."

His parents have taken all of his decisions in stride, from learning to skydive, to returning to skydiving after a plane crash nearly took his life. "I am my mother's only child," Will explained. "She's incredibly supportive, as in 'you gotta live your life and not in fear.'" His mom comes out to the drop zone from time to time to watch, and the drop zone owner who also pilots

or copilots their new Cessna will occasionally send his mom photos of Will sleeping in the back of the aircraft. "My mom loves those pictures," said Will. "She still has them on her phone."

Seat belts must be worn for all Takeoffs & Landings
Door must be latched closed for all takeoffs and landings.
Maximum door opening and closing speed, 80 MPH IAS.
Maximum speed with the door open 100 MPH IAS.
All loose objects in the cabin must be secured.
Jumper static line must be installed in a manner to prevent
interference with the aircraft control surfaces.
Pilot shall wear a parachute and observers carried during
a jumping operation shall wear a parachute.

Will Grow Anywhere

featuring Chrisha Favors

EUGENE, OREGON

CONFEDERATED TRIBES OF SILETZ INDIANS, CONFEDERATED TRIBES OF GRAND RONDE, KALAPUYA, WINEFELLY, CHELAMELA

CHRISHA FAVORS'S RELATIONSHIP TO THE OUTDOORS REACHES BACK to her grandfather, who inspired her sense of connection to nature. Growing up in South Georgia, she spent a lot of time exploring the trails on his land, collecting fresh eggs from the chicken coop, and gardening.

Her other interest was music. Chrisha obtained a bachelor's degree in music from Valdosta State University in 2008 and gave private lessons in woodwinds, brass, piano, and voice.

When she and her husband moved to California in 2015, she began volunteering with outdoor nonprofits and eventually found a position as an environmental educator. One program focused on Latinx kids from underserved communities, and the other focused on mostly upper-middle-class kids. It was a lot to take in for Chrisha, who was also intent on taking up space as a Black woman in a predominantly white field. "On the one hand, I was trying to help kids realize that they belonged in these spaces, and on the other hand I was working with absolutely rich kids who knew everything about nature," said Chrisha.

She isn't new to the challenges that stem from being a Black woman in a predominantly white field. Growing up, Chrisha had a difficult time connecting with other Black kids. Part of it had to do with her interests—choir ensembles and community bands—but part of it had to do with the racism she had internalized as a child. "I had this fear of being viewed as ghetto when I was younger," said Chrisha. "I didn't want to be viewed as 'poor' or 'Black' or any of the things that I told myself were negative at the time. Even though my parents were very pro-Black, for me, all of my friends were white and I wanted to be like them."

Chrisha and her husband recently moved to Oregon, where they purchased a home on thirteen acres. After years of tending potted plants and raised bed planters, she's putting down literal roots in the soil of their new home. "I've had my own garden since 2009," she explained. "I've grown tomatoes, cucumbers, sweet peas, peppers, broccoli—which turned out okay—lettuce and collard greens, my favorite." Her grandfather was behind the vision for their current homestead, which backs up to a 300-acre nature preserve.

Moving to the Pacific Northwest also inspired her to get more into foraging. Although she's mostly self-taught, she has taken a few classes "to feel confident in what I'm foraging and make sure it's absolutely edible before I put it in my mouth." She forages for mushrooms, yucca, and other edible plants. "It's all about empowerment," Chrisha added. She also finds a lot of encouragement and community from following hashtags on social media like #BlackGirlsGarden.

Her advice to first-time gardeners is to visit your local nursery to see what's in season. "They usually have starts—tomatoes, peppers, and beans, which are the easiest thing to grow," Chrisha advised. "They look cool, they trellis, and you can get a good yield from one start. They also do really well in pots and will grow anywhere."

Acknowledgments

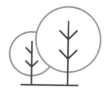

I OWE AN ENORMOUS DEBT OF GRATITUDE TO MY SISTER DR. LOGAN Williams for pushing, pulling, and patiently encouraging me to finish this book while I was hospitalized and recovering from meningitis, blood clots, and an anesthesia allergy. Thank you for keeping communication lines open with my editor and for nudging me to do my best each day. Thanks for making the impossible possible.

Many thanks are owed to Eric Arce, the official book photographer who captured many of the amazing images featured within. Thank you for breathing life into so many different stories with beautiful, dynamic photos of gravity-defying athletes.

I will forever be indebted to my assistant Shi-Lynn Campbell who worked nonstop through the winter holidays to help me license many of the breath-taking images featured here.

I appreciate each and every individual who entrusted me with their story. The #MelaninBaseCamp and #DiversifyOutdoors communities are so expansive. This is not an exhaustive list of people by any means, but I am honored to be able to share the stories contained within.

Last but not least, I would like to acknowledge the team at Black Dog & Leventhal for believing in this project from day one. Thank you for helping to build a more inclusive and equitable outdoors.

Notes

RUNNING FOR HEALING AND SOCIAL CHANGE

page 41 *Violence Against Women Reauthorization Act:* National Institute of Justice, "Violence Against Women Act (VAWA) Reauthorization 2013." Accessed September 1, 2021. https://www.justice.gov/tribal/violence-against-women-act-vawa-reauthorization-2013-0.

page 41 *four out of five Native women experience violence, including sexual violence, physical violence, and stalking:* National Institute of Justice, "Violence Against American Indian and Alaska Native Women and Men." Accessed September 1, 2021. https://nij.ojp.gov/topics/articles/violence-against-american-indian-and-alaska-native-women-and-men.

page 41 *overwhelmingly by non-Native perpetrators:* National Institute of Justice, "Figure 1: Estimates of Lifetime Interracial and Intraracial Violence." Accessed September 1, 2021. https://nij.ojp.gov/media/image/19456.

page 44 *A resolution was finally passed in 2021:* Congress.gov, "Text: H.R.1319–117th Congress (2021–2022)." Accessed September 1, 2021. https://www.congress.gov/bill/117th-congress/house-bill/1319/text.

LEARNING TO FLY

page 49 *"It's a suit that becomes pressurized…and gives you the feeling of actually flying":* Danielle Williams, Team Blackstar Featured Athletes: Brandon. Accessed September 1, 2021. https://www.teamblackstar.com/featured-bj.

page 49 *"I've got a bit of a fascination with space and decided that I wanted my wingsuit to reflect that":* Ibid.

page 52 *"BASE jumping involves jumping from a fixed object…There are no backups, so the risk is a lot higher":* Ibid.

GUIDE TO OUTDOOR ALLYSHIP: PART 2—SELF-AWARENESS

page 81 *a white Kampgrounds of America employee pulled a gun on them:* Elliott McLaughlin, "She Was Fired for Pulling a Gun on a Black Couple. Now, the Ex-Campground Employee Has Been Arrested," CNN, June 5, 2019. https://www.cnn.com/2019/06/04/us/kampgrounds-of-america-employee-arrested-gun/index.html.

page 81 *Black attorney pushing his son in a stroller…was flagged by police after a white woman reported a "suspicious man walking the bike path with a baby":* Brian Tyler Cohen, "A Black Dad Just Took His Baby Son on a Stroll in the Park. Then, a White Woman Freaked Out," *Washington Press*, May 16, 2018. https://washingtonpress.com/2018/05/16/a-black-dad-just-took-his-baby-son-on-a-stroll-in-the-park-then-a-white-woman-freaked-out/.

THE ONLY BLACK BACKPACKER ON THE TRAIL

page 127 *Chilkoot Trail:* National Park Service, "Explore the Chilkoot Trail–Klondike Gold Rush National Historical Park (U.S. National Park Service)," December 31, 2019. https://www.nps.gov/klgo/planyourvisit/chilkoottrail.htm.

page 127 *Allagash Wilderness Waterway:* Allagash Wilderness Waterway, "Guide & Map." Accessed September 1, 2021. https://www.maine.gov/dacf/parksearch/PropertyGuides/PDF_GUIDE/aww-guide.pdf.

page 127 *Agiocochook or Mount Washington, receives nearly 280,000 visitors annually:* "100+ Things to Know About NH's Mount Washington," *New Hampshire Magazine*. Accessed September 1, 2021. https://www.nhmagazine.com/mount-washington/.

page 127 *"highest wind speed ever recorded in the world (231 mph)":* "Wild Weather and the Mt. Washington Observatory," *New Hampshire Magazine*, May 9, 2019. https://www.nhmagazine.com/wild-weather-and-the-mount-washington-observatory/.

About the Author

DANIELLE WILLIAMS IS FOUNDER OF DIVERSIFYOUTDOORS.COM AND Senior Editor of MelaninBaseCamp.com. Her love of adventure sports began in 2006 when the U.S. Army threw her out of her first airplane. Since 2016, she's worked to increase the visibility of outdoorsy individuals from BIPOC, LGBTQ+, and disabled communities. In 2018, she founded #DiversifyOutdoors, a coalition of digital influencers, affinity groups, and allies leveraging the power of social networks to build a more inclusive and equitable outdoors. Danielle has been featured in Vogue Business, Refinery29, NPR, *New York Times*, ABC News, Hulu, and more. On the weekends you can find her hiking, skydiving, or doing nothing at all because she deserves rest and so do you!

Photo Credits

Pages 3, 7, 10, 13, 57, 65, 93, 135, 171, 235, 238, 240: Photographs by limeart via Getty Images; Pages 4-5: Photograph by Cheyenne Smith, copyright © MBC; Page 6: Photographs by Eric Arce, copyright © MBC; Page 9: Photograph copyright © Michael Pang; Page 12: Photographs by Eric Arce, copyright © MBC; Page 14: Photograph copyright © Verna Volker; Page 16: Photograph copyright © Danielle Williams; Pages 17, 27, 39, 73, 85, 103, 109, 127, 155, 163, 177, 183, 193, 207: Photographs by appleuzr via Getty Images; Pages 18-19: Photograph copyright © Chad Wilcox; Pages: 21-25: Photograph copyright © Danielle Williams; Pages 26, 28-29, 30: Photograph copyright © Yibin Zhang; Page 31: Photograph copyright © Clint Clayton; Pages 32-35: Photograph copyright © Yibin Zhang; Pages 36-37: Photograph copyright © Mike Zubelewicz; Pages 38, 40, 42-43, 44-45, 46-47: Photograph copyright © Verna Volker; Pages 48, 50-51: Photograph copyright © Nicholas Scalabrino; Pages 49, 147, 217: Photographs by Nadiinko via Getty Images; Pages 52, 53, 54-55: Photograph copyright © Andrew Ford; Pages 56, 59, 60-61, 62, 63: Photographs by Eric Arce, copyright © MBC; Pages 64, 66-67, 68-69, 70-71: Photograph copyright © Cheyenne Smith; Pages 72, 75, 76-77, 78-79: Photograph copyright © Ted Borland; Page 80: Photograph copyright © Danielle Williams; Pages 84, 89, 90: Photograph copyright © Rick Teudt; Pages 86-87: Photograph copyright © Mushtaque Silat; Pages 92, 94-95, 96, 97, 98, 100-101: Photograph copyright © Priscilla Macy-Cruser; Pages 102, 104-105, 107: Photograph copyright © Michael Pang; Pages 108, 110-111, 112, 113, 114: Photographs by Eric Arce, copyright © MBC; Pages 116, 118-119, 120-121, 122, 124-125: Photograph copyright © George Stephens; Page 126: Photograph copyright © Klementovich; Pages 128-129: Photograph copyright © Paula Champagne; Pages 130, 132-133: Photograph copyright © Klementovich; Pages 134, 136-137, 139, 140-141: Photographs by Eric Arce, copyright © MBC; Page 142: Photograph copyright © Danielle Williams; Page 145: Photograph by Eric Arce, copyright © MBC; Page 146: Photograph copyright © Elliot Byrd; Pages 148-149: Photograph copyright © David Cherry; Pages 150-151: Photograph copyright © David Wybenga; Page 152: Photograph copyright © David Cherry; Pages 154, 156, 157, 158-159, 160-161: Photographs by Eric Arce, copyright © MBC; Pages 162, 164-165, 167, 168-169: Photograph copyright © Yani Palencia; Page 170: Photograph copyright © Zach Brazle; Page 173: Photograph copyright © Sebastian Marin; Page 174: Photograph copyright © Evan Woodward; Pages 176, 178, 180-181: Photograph copyright © Johnathan Malik Martin; Pages 182, 184, 185, 187, 188-189, 190: Photographs by Eric Arce, copyright © MBC; Pages 191, 192, 194, 195, 196-197, 199, 200-201: Photograph copyright © Michael Estrada; Pages 206, 208-209, 210, 213, 214-215: Photographs by Eric Arce, copyright © MBC; Pages 216, 218-219, 220, 222-223, 224-225: Photograph copyright © Michael Turner; Pages 226, 228, 229, 230-231, 232-233: Photograph copyright © Chrisha Favors; Pages 234, 235: Photograph copyright © Danielle Williams